D0054227

THE
GOLDEN
MOTORCYCLE
GANG

HAY HOUSE TITLES OF RELATED INTEREST

YOU CAN HEAL YOUR LIFE, the movie,
starring Louise L. Hay & Friends
(available as a 1-DVD program and an expanded 2-DVD set)
Watch the trailer at: **www.LouiseHayMovie.com**

THE SHIFT, the movie, starring Dr. Wayne W. Dyer
(available as a 1-DVD program and an expanded 2-DVD set)
Watch the trailer at: **www.DyerMovie.com**

*THE FIRST RULE OF TEN: Book One of the Dharma
Detective Series,* by Gay Hendricks and Tinker Lindsay
(available January 2012)

FRACTAL TIME: The Secret of 2012 and a New World Age,
by Gregg Braden

THE LAST DROPOUT: <u>Stop</u> the Epidemic! by Bill Milliken

SIMPLY GENIUS! And Other Tales from My Life,
by Ervin Laszlo

*THIS IS THE MOMENT! How One Man's Yearlong
Journey Captured the Power of Extraordinary Gratitude,*
by Walter Green

All of the above are available at your local bookstore,
or may be ordered by visiting:

Hay House USA: **www.hayhouse.com**®
Hay House Australia: **www.hayhouse.com.au**
Hay House UK: **www.hayhouse.co.uk**
Hay House South Africa: **www.hayhouse.co.za**
Hay House India: **www.hayhouse.co.in**

THE
GOLDEN
MOTORCYCLE
GANG

A STORY OF TRANSFORMATION

JACK CANFIELD
WILLIAM GLADSTONE

HAY HOUSE, INC.
Carlsbad, California • New York City
London • Sydney • Johannesburg
Vancouver • Hong Kong • New Delhi

Published and distributed in the United States by: Hay House, Inc.: www
.hayhouse.com • *Published and distributed in Australia by:* Hay House
Australia Pty. Ltd.: www.hayhouse.com.au • *Published and distributed
in the United Kingdom by:* Hay House UK, Ltd.: www.hayhouse.co.uk •
Published and distributed in the Republic of South Africa by: Hay House
SA (Pty), Ltd.: www.hayhouse.co.za • *Distributed in Canada by:* Raincoast:
www.raincoast.com • *Published in India by:* Hay House Publishers India:
www.hayhouse.co.in

Editorial supervision: Jill Kramer • *Project editor:* Shannon Littrell
Cover design: Christy Salinas • *Interior design:* Tricia Breidenthal

4764 1070 1/12

Library of Congress Cataloging-in-Publication Data

Canfield, Jack.
  The Golden Motorcycle Gang : a story of transformation / Jack Canfield and
William Gladstone. -- 1st ed.
      p. cm.
  Includes bibliographical references.
  ISBN 978-1-4019-3619-8 (hardcover : alk. paper) 1. Spirituality. 2. Human
evolution--Miscellanea. 3. Prophecies (Occultism) 4. Civilization--Forecast-
ing. 5. Civilization--20th century. 6. Civilization--21st century. I. Glad-
stone, William, 1949- II. Title.
  BF1999.C275 2011
  204--dc23

                                    2011027795

Hardcover ISBN: 978-1-4019-3619-8
Digital ISBN: 978-1-4019-3620-4

14 13 12 11   4 3 2 1
1st edition, November 2011

Printed in the United States of America

CONTENTS

VIDEO MESSAGE FROM
William Gladstone

SNAP A MOBILE PIC

Ez.com/wgladstone

NEED MOBILE READER?
EZ.com/getreader

FOREWORD

On a beautiful Santa Barbara, California, day in 2011, at 5:00 P.M., three evolutionary thinkers of our time met at the Boathouse restaurant. Following a discussion of cosmic proportions, they began planning a birthday party: yours, mine, *humanity's birthday party!* The invitation could read as follows:

> *You are lovingly invited to celebrate the birth of Universal Humanity. Join us in creating a life-affirming future for all beings upon Earth.*
>
> **Date:** *December 22, 2012*
> **Time:** *Beginning Midnight, December 21, 2012*
> **Place:** *Throughout the Planet*
> *Bring as many guests as you wish!*

Vision without action is a fantasy.
Action without vision is chaos.

The Golden, Silver, and Diamond Motorcycle Gangs; and the Transformational Leadership Council are what "visionary action" looks like. They provide inspired, practical answers to the questions pulling at both our consciousness and our conscience: Will our collective human future include the emergence of our highest evolutionary purpose and potential? Are there enough individuals willing to become agents for change and accelerate the evolutionary agenda for the planet?

Every day we have 86,400 seconds of opportunity to contribute to the emergence of our individual and collective awakening. If you Google "collective consciousness," you'll get more than 64,000 results referencing terms such as *collective mind, co-creative society, collective resonance,* and *group mind.* These results point to evidence that there is a growing recognition of how a collective vision builds momentum, magnetizing like-minded individuals into its orbit. Once gathered in this unified field of consciousness, possibilities beyond our grandest individual vision give way to the power of the Whole.

The great Hindu philosopher Sri Aurobindo realized the awesome power of the collective consciousness and its impact on our planet's evolutionary progress when he wrote: "All will be united by the evolution of the Truth-Consciousness in them; in the changed way of being which this consciousness would bring about in them, they will feel themselves to be embodiments of a single self, souls of a single Reality; illumined and motivated by a fundamental unity of knowledge, actuated by a fundamental unified will and feeling."

May all of you who read Jack and Bill's *Golden Motorcycle Gang* become confidently optimistic about your individual capacity to bring about global change. Whether through the workshops or organizations described in the appendices, or another group dedicated to celebrating our collective identity and destiny, may each of you respond with a resounding "yes" to the invitation.

The Golden Motorcycle Gang is a story that is not only easy to read, it is filled with insights into the dawning of a transformative reality for our planet. So, grab your keys to consciousness, put on your helmet of wisdom, and get ready to ride into the winds of planetary transformation.

— **Michael Bernard Beckwith**
Los Angeles, California

INTRODUCTION

*"I am like a little pencil in
[God's] hand. That is all."*

— MOTHER TERESA

The Golden Motorcycle Gang is a unique book. Although written as a fictional account of the life of Jack Canfield, we have for the most part used names of real people and actual incidents from Jack's life. We have taken liberties with timing and other elements to create a coherent story line. We have created dialogues that in some instances never actually occurred, but which capture the essence of special moments and relationships in Jack's life. It has often been stated that truth is stranger than fiction. In the case of *The Golden*

Motorcycle Gang, we expect you will find that truth is often contained *within* fiction.

As authors, we are delighted that you have chosen to read this book. We believe that the world has reached a tipping point, and that it is time for each and every one of us to "show up." We remain optimistic that war, global warming, natural catastrophes, greed, corruption, and other ills will not overwhelm the ultimate destiny prophesied in most major religions and cultures around the world: that human beings are in fact destined to live in a better world in the 21st century.

This better world, of course, requires that the material side of life—access to clean water, healthy food, shelter, good education, and opportunities to create —be well maintained. But to achieve these material results we must also address the spiritual values, which are the foundation of any great civilization and certainly a planetary global civilization in which all people are interconnected. No single individual can be left behind in this great adventure. We are all part of one consciousness and one world.

Think of yourself as a single cell in a great body. Is one cell more important than any other for that body to function? We might think a brain cell or a heart cell has more value, but the reality is if a majority of liver cells or lung cells are not functioning, the body will not function. In 1 Corinthians 12: 12–14, it is written:

> For as the body is one, and hath many members, and all the members of that one body, being many, are one body: so also is Christ. For by one Spirit are we all baptized into one body, whether we be Jews or Gentiles, whether we be bond or free; and have been all made to drink into one Spirit. For the body is not one member, but many.

These words embody the eternal truth that exists in all authentic religious and spiritual teachings. Each and every one of us has a role to play, and on the highest spiritual level we must work in unison like cells in a single body, for we are in reality all one. Yet what is unique about our invitation to you, our readers, is not just to remind you of this eternal truth—but to draw your attention to the reality that time is in fact running out. Based on the teachings of our visionary friend Barbara Marx Hubbard, we have come to appreciate what she calls Conscious Evolution.

Conscious Evolution is most simply described as "evolution by choice, not chance." As evolved intelligent beings, we can for the first time on planet Earth choose the course of evolution. If we choose wisely, we can collectively create what many might consider "heaven on Earth." Should we choose poorly, however, we may create the kind of catastrophes that will set back evolution on planet Earth for thousands of years.

Scientists are reporting that there is unity throughout the universe in ways never before realized. Many believe that there is direction and purpose to evolution throughout the universe, an innate desire in the process of creativity itself to self-organize and create ever more complex organizations and patterns of beauty. We cannot assure you that this is true, but we know from our life experiences that working toward the good and the benefit of others is perhaps the greatest reward any of us can have while in a human body.

Through the metaphor of the Golden Motorcycle Gang, we hope to awaken you to your own highest calling. Together, we believe, we can make a difference. To facilitate this we have included appendices that list organizations with which you can become involved to literally "join the gang."

The appendices list organizations and people who are working toward the positive transformation of our planet. We felt it important to provide specific contact information for, and in some cases brief descriptions of, these organizations, because our goal in writing *The Golden Motorcycle Gang* is not just to entertain you, but to inspire you to take action that will improve your life and the lives of others. The second decade of the 21st century is likely to be a pivotal decade for our planet. We encourage you to marvel at the miracle of being alive at this specific time, and at your ability to make a positive difference for generations to come.

In this book you will learn many details about the life of Jack Canfield. We are providing this background because we think Jack is an example of what may be true for each and every one of us: that we all have a divine purpose, and that we all incarnated with a special mission to accomplish that purpose. When he was younger, Jack did not know what his mission was meant to be. In some ways he is still learning the details of that mission. It is in the details of his life, the often seemingly unimportant "random connections" of living on a certain street or meeting a certain person at a particular time that continually pointed Jack toward his destiny. We believe that this is true for you and everyone else as well.

Scientific research has just begun on what in the past have been considered "coincidences" and synchronicity. Scientists are now learning that what we consider synchronicity is often part of a larger life plan that is part of a larger design, and potentially evolution's purpose. Dr. Gary Schwartz of the University of Arizona is one of the leading researchers in this new field of study. His research reports that people often receive repeated signs of what they are supposed to be doing and with whom they should be connecting. Unfortunately, these signs are too often ignored, leaving people's sense of purpose and accomplishment less than fulfilled.

One of our goals in writing *The Golden Motorcycle Gang* is to let you see how the process of synchronicity works in the specific case of Jack Canfield. Bill Gladstone has written a novel called *The Twelve* in which, based on his actual life experiences, he explores the role of synchronicity in his own life—and how his life is connected to the prophecies related to the end of the Mayan calendar on December 21, 2012. Both Bill and Jack feel that the writing of this book came about because of synchronicities that have directed their life purpose. Barbara Marx Hubbard has been a major influence on both Jack and Bill, and she too has felt the pull of her life purpose in incidents large and small.

There is something special about the times in which we are living, and our hope is that you start to pay attention—as Jack, Bill, and Barbara have—to the signs and critical moments that helped each of them uncover their life purpose. A pattern is coming together on planet Earth at this precise moment. You are part of this pattern. It may be that through seemingly insignificant details and coincidences, you will discover your specific role in the evolution of the universe.

Sit back and enjoy the tale of the Golden Motorcycle Gang.

PRELUDE

November 22, 1943

"The master gave his teaching in parables
and stories, which his disciples listened to with
pleasure—and occasional frustration, for
they longed for something deeper.

"The master was unmoved. To all their
objections he would say, 'You have yet to understand,
my dears, that the shortest distance between
a human being and truth is a story.'"

— ANTHONY DE MELLO

On a cold morning in Warsaw, Emily was excited as she awoke. Today she would be six years old; and although her parents had warned her many times not to go into the street outside of their building, she could hear so much noise and activity that she could not stay behind the old stone wall.

Emily opened the front door to the family's apartment only a little, and before it creaked, slid through and quietly walked toward the wall. Could other people be celebrating her birthday as well? She followed the path up the wall that she'd seen the older boys climb, and her eyes just crested over the wall.

Emily saw trucks with soldiers sitting inside, stiff and upright like wooden toys, and even more soldiers marching next to the trucks. And people, so many people, marching behind the soldiers—and then even more trucks and soldiers behind them. Any of the people who stepped out of line or stumbled were yelled at, and some were even beaten by the soldiers with the ends of their guns. The people were so dirty and sad. Many of them, even the men, were crying.

What did those people do that was so bad? Emily wondered.

"Emily, get down from that wall right now!" her mother ordered in a quiet but furious shout, as she burst through the front door and hurled herself to-ward the wall to collect her daughter.

In Japan, nine-year-old Hiro cried as his father, Emoto, embraced him one last time. "You know I must go off to war. I may not see you for a long time. You must be brave. You are the man of the house now."

In the quiet of early evening, Hiro had heard the zippers and buckles fastening from his parents' bedroom, which always meant his father was going away, but this time it was different. His father's tightly lined mouth, the way he held Hiro's head more firmly than usual as they hugged, and the papers that Hiro had seen on the table—orders for his father to leave immediately to join the Imperial Japanese Army—told Hiro that this time was very different.

In London, eight-year-old Paul was tired. It seemed that he was always tired. Almost two years had passed since the last German bombings in London, but the terror had lasted longer than the frenzied rush to the shelters, the thunderous booming, the blackened air, and even the crying. He had never been able to put the sound of the air-raid sirens out of his mind, not for an evening. He heard it in his dreams, in his nightmares, and even as he lay awake at night. Any ambulance he heard wailing made his mind go back to those nights in hell.

Paul's parents had tried to comfort him and had done what they could to make him feel safe, but he could not forget the sounds or what he had seen when they had last emerged from the shelter two years ago. His home and those of his neighbors had been destroyed in the fires created by the bombs. Everything he knew in the world—his toys, his books, his favorite shoes—had been destroyed.

The most devastating loss of all was Paul's beloved kitten, Penelope. The family hadn't had time to gather her before going into the shelter, and she was nowhere to be found.

After the bombing, Paul couldn't walk the streets without thinking he saw Penelope crouching behind this door or curling up on the ledge in that window. He just could not accept that she was gone.

THROUGHOUT THE UNIVERSE

*"The purpose of
life is a life of purpose."*

— ROBERT BYRNE

Oh, what glorious beings they were! Flying through the universe on their magnificent golden motorcycles, the cosmic wind in their hair, going wherever they chose, traveling at light speed, sometimes even faster. Their bodies were ephemeral yet defined, and they enjoyed the ageless youth gifted to their species. Only a few thousand years old, they were considered adolescents, not yet the elders of their planet or their universe—elders who each had tens of thousands of years of experience in dealing with complex worlds and the moral difficulties that arose from engaging those worlds.

The beings traveled through this beautiful, endless day, which was much like the many they'd enjoyed together on their annual solstice breaks. As the Class of 2012 at the Academy of Enlightenment, they were fast approaching the time when they would graduate and be given assignments to ensure the balance and stability of the universe for eons to come, much like their elders before them. Today, however, was a day to enjoy the carefree exhilaration of their youth and freedom.

Dozens of them rode together, sharing their boundless joy through their thoughts, for they communicated only with thoughts. Their thoughts shaped words, which they immediately understood; yet communication was instantaneous, faster than words could ever be, and infinitely more clear.

It was a perfect day and they were in high spirits. Suddenly Jack noticed a small bluish planet off to his right. It was about 50,000 miles below but clearly visible to him. "Hey, look over there. That planet seems to be in trouble. I can sense the energy coming from the surface—and it's full of turmoil, sadness, anger, even rage. I've seen this planet before; I have sensed its people and their growth and their struggles. Although there have always been some discordant sparks from

2

this world, I've never felt such sorrow as I'm feeling today." Such was Jack's instantaneous thought to his riding friends, or as they liked to call themselves, the Golden Motorcycle Gang.

On that magical motorcycle ride through the universe, Jack and his friends had easily picked up on the negative energy coming from planet Earth. The suffering radiating from the dazzling blue ball was unmistakable.

The year on Earth was 1943, and great conflict was raging on much of the planet. The battles engulfed a great deal of its middle band, from one great ocean to the next. The planet was divided into groups called "nations," which were sometimes the result of geography but oftentimes the result of human choice. Many of the largest and most militarily well-armed nations were focused on the fighting. Almost all the human beings on the planet at that time were thinking about this great conflict, whether their nation would exist if and when the battles ever ended, and if their loved ones would survive and return from the battlefields around the world.

Jack looked around and realized that for perhaps the only time in his existence, he had no explanation for the energy being emitted by this planet. What was this "war," as the humans called it? What in a human's

3

life could happen that would convince him or her that it was right and good to end the lives of millions of other identically created life-forms?

Jack decided he needed to learn as much as he could, as quickly as he could, about this concept of "war." War was not a reality in the outer reaches of the universe where he lived, and although he lacked the understanding of the impulse to hate and kill, he knew he would not be able to help planet Earth unless he learned more about war and the decision to kill others.

"Yes, what a tragedy," his close friend Michael thought back. "Such a beautiful blue planet, so full of life, creativity, and joy despite the clear tumors that seem to be infesting it now."

"Tumors? I never thought of these ills as tumors, but that planet needs some help," Jack thought back to Michael. "I think we should do something. All our decades of training at the Academy of Enlightenment have prepared us for our roles as masters of harmony. I think we should stop by this planet and see what we can do to help."

Mark, another member of the Gang, looked at Jack in disbelief. "Jack, this is the first day of our solstice break. We have a great voyage ahead of us. We can go anywhere and everywhere, no responsibilities,

4

no fixed agenda, just experiencing all that the universe has to offer and the solidarity of great friends. Do you know how long it might take to get that little blue globe back on track? It could take us several human lifetimes or more, and that would certainly put a damper on our fun."

"That may be so, but look at them," Jack replied. "They're slowly destroying themselves. They're in real trouble. Think how great it would be to get that planet back into balance. I have tuned in to it, and it is a really special place—with many different species and lots of variety with respect to geography, climate, and creative ideas. It could be a really fun place. And, what's most ironic is that it's their wonderful diversity that is dividing them into opposing factions and threatening their continued existence. What makes them so special is also what's causing them to face extinction.

"The people there call their planet 'Earth.' There has only been intelligent life on Earth for ten or twenty thousand years. That planet is not much older than we are. We should take a little time to see if we can prevent the catastrophic events that we can sense are ahead for them. I think it would be an adventure . . . and when we get back to the Academy, if we can get this Earth back to health, we would probably get all kinds of extra credit for it." Jack added this overly optimistic goal, knowing it would probably appeal to his fellow riders.

"Well, since you put it that way, I can't let you go alone," Mark shot back. "So if you're bound and determined to go down there, I guess we're all going to have to join you."

"Absolutely," beamed Michael and Janet; along with Steve, Bob, Martin, and Marcia. The rest of the Golden Motorcycle Gang silently voiced their approval. Mission accepted!

In what seemed to them no more than the blink of an eye, each had taken form as new beings—"human beings," born on planet Earth.

The Gang had failed to mention one critical element of their mission of intervention and redemption: once they were born into human bodies, they would forget that they were cosmic beings with unlimited lifetimes. In order to grow and develop as human beings on Earth, many years would pass before they would remember who they truly were and why they had chosen to be born into a body.

And so our story of the Golden Motorcycle Gang and their adventures on planet Earth begins.

WHO IS JACK?

*"A journey of a thousand miles
begins with one step."*

— LAO-TZU

"It's a boy."

The words of the doctor, and an unexpected physical pain in the dense little body that he now inhabited, were the last things Jack would remember before a new human consciousness took hold of his being. Jack was born on August 19, 1944, a sultry summer day, to a 20-year-old American beauty, Ellen Canfield, in Fort Worth, Texas. Gone was the awareness of the whys and hows of becoming human. Jack immediately started to forget who he was and why he had decided to be born as a human being.

And so, he became . . . human.

United States Air Force first lieutenant Bud Canfield, on leave four days after Jack's birth, greeted his infant son with a tremendous whooping laugh, a hug covering him from head to toe, and a sturdy wooden model of the P-38 Lightning airplane that Bud had carefully put together by hand during the long bus ride to Fort Worth from his base. Bud was only 24 years old but more proud of his son than he could have ever imagined, and even more excited that his firstborn was a boy. Bud's working-class family had a strong tradition of military service, and although he knew his newborn was too small to play with a model airplane, he wanted that plane in Jack's hands in the event Bud didn't make it back from a future overseas assignment.

For Bud, defending his country was the highest possible calling, and he wanted his son to respect this tradition—and to know that even if his father couldn't be with Jack to teach him what it meant to serve his country, the model airplane would remind him throughout his life of the family's military traditions, along with the honor found in protecting their homeland.

Bud's abilities as a pilot earned him the right to train other B-17 bomber pilots, so he was repeatedly transferred to military bases throughout the United States. The Air Force was playing an increasingly important role in the American war effort, and his expertise was in heavy demand throughout the training bases in the U.S. Bud's work was critical to the war effort, but he found that he lost focus when he was away from Ellen and his son. So each time he was reassigned, he took his family along with him.

In a period of just two years, Jack lived in Omaha, Minneapolis, and several other cities throughout the United States. After the U.S. and her allies won the war, Bud was offered the opportunity to apply his technical and managerial skills to selling automobile parts in the town of Wheeling, West Virginia. The position paid much more than did the military, and Ellen had family in the area. Wheeling was in many ways a postcard-perfect American town. With only 35,000 people and the beauty of nature to be found in every direction, both Ellen and Bud felt they had found the ideal place to raise their family.

Jack had no memory of why he'd decided to be born as a human, and he had no recollection of the Golden Motorcycle Gang. He was conscious, however, of the way his body was growing (and how quickly he grew), and of how his hands deftly served so many different purposes. He didn't share these thoughts with anybody; he just figured they were the thoughts of most little boys.

Ellen, although a strict mother, was always hugging Jack and his younger brothers, telling them how much she loved them. The boys enjoyed exploring their neighborhood streams and woods, which, along with the Ohio River, made up their modest but comfortable childhood world.

For much of the adult population of Wheeling in the postwar period, drinking was one of the primary methods of relaxation. Ellen was a moderate drinker, mostly during multifamily picnics or other social events, but Bud's habits were different.

Once he started drinking, Bud could drain almost an entire bottle of whiskey in one evening. And when he drank too much, he was often cruel and violent with his wife and sons. When sober, Bud was strict and a highly demanding father. He believed in physical discipline, and he didn't hesitate to spank Jack when his son misbehaved. When Bud drank, things got worse.

Bud would spank Jack with a heavy pig-bristle hairbrush, which hurt and stung more than any hand ever could. Jack, after a few such spankings, became terrified of his father and would hide whenever he thought he was in trouble or when Bud had been drinking. Jack became very adept at hiding, even figuring out a way to conceal himself in the bottom of an old console radio that his father would never consider as a possible hiding place. Bud would rage around the house looking for Jack, and although he knew he was only delaying the inevitable, Jack had learned that Bud's fury would eventually lessen—and, in most instances, so would the intensity of the spankings.

Bud Canfield was out of the military, but the military was in no way out of him. He held firm to the strict ideals of order, discipline, hierarchy, and, most of all, rules. Bud had all manner of rules: If Jack or his brothers didn't eat all of their dinner, including their vegetables, they wouldn't be given any dessert. If they didn't keep their rooms clean, they were "grounded," unable leave the house except for school. And one of Bud's most important commandments was being on time for all appointments.

As a little boy, Jack loved nature, sports, and playing in the forest around his house. He imagined he was somehow a pioneer, exploring this area for the first time, seeing what nobody before him had ever seen.

He would often get caught up in the slightest distraction, such as quietly following a butterfly as it flew from flower to flower, or a squirrel as it ran and hopped from tree to tree. Jack's focus during his hidden pursuits was singular, and nothing in the world mattered so much to him as that these creatures would make it back to their homes and families. Sometimes only darkness would bring the boy home, and he would be as much as an hour late for dinner. Bud would be upset, and while he wouldn't always spank him, Jack could count on being punished in some way.

A few months after his sixth birthday, Jack's life changed. Bud's drinking had worsened to the point that Ellen decided she could not live with him any longer. She filed for divorce, and she and her three sons moved in with her mother while she sorted out her life without Bud.

Jack's grandmother Blanche ran a small gift shop from her home. She sold cashmere sweaters, imported soaps, silver picture frames, and other special gift items to friends and neighbors. Jack loved seeing all the people stopping by his new home, and he loved running around free and without fear. The swirl of activity around the house, along with his grandmother's ability to turn seemingly ordinary (and to his young eyes, frequently odd) items into gifts that delighted people and also made money, fascinated Jack. The young boy quickly found that he wanted to be like his grandmother. He wanted to make people happy and earn a great living at the same time.

Although he was then only eight years old, Jack became a junior entrepreneur. He discovered a way to make money by helping out in his neighborhood. Just two blocks away from his new home was a park with a hand pump that yielded fresh springwater. Jack would fill one-gallon containers with the sweet springwater, put them in his bright-colored red wagon, and wheel the containers to the homes of several elderly widows who were most grateful for Jack's assistance. They would pay Jack a nickel or a dime for his efforts, and in a single day, he would earn enough to attend the Saturday-matinee movies he so dearly loved.

His early success with pumping and delivering water inspired Jack to get a newspaper route. Soon he could be seen throughout the neighborhood, speeding along on his bicycle, practicing his newspaper toss as he skillfully maneuvered between parked cars, barking dogs, and stray roller skates on the sidewalks. Jack loved the feel of the air rushing through his hair and would pedal as fast as possible—not just so he could finish his route more quickly, but simply for the physical thrill of speed.

Jack enjoyed the ideal childhood he had largely missed in his earlier years in the house ruled by his father's unforgiving nature. After about a year of living with Blanche, Ellen remarried. Jack and his brothers left their grandmother's home and moved in with their new stepdad, Fred. Soon, the boys had a little sister, Kim.

Jack still saw his father, Bud, occasionally, but Fred was around for Jack every day and became what Jack considered his "real" dad.

By the age of ten, Jack excelled in school and sports and had lots of friends. His relationship with his mother grew closer and healthier, as they'd both escaped Bud's temper and his rules. And although Fred and Ellen had limited financial resources, Jack had a wealthy great-aunt who saw promise in him and arranged for him to start the fifth grade at a private military school in Wheeling. He continued to do well in his studies, and made a seamless transition to becoming a teenager.

Jack's teenage years revolved around school and his prowess in sports, and they were a wonderful time for him. He played football and made the prestigious

Wheeling All-City Team as an "end," which in high-school games of that era was the player to whom many passes were thrown. In Jack's case, the passes often resulted in touchdowns. He was also a member of the swim team, ran the quarter-mile and the mile relay for the track team, sang in the glee club, and was generally quite popular in school.

The glee club was really special to Jack. He loved the ability to create harmony with others through song, and was inspired to learn to play the guitar. During his junior year, he joined with friends in forming their own musical group—soon he was singing songs about peace, love, banning the bomb, social injustice, and the other causes of the early 1960s. Often during these musical sessions, Jack experienced transcendent moments of unity and joy.

It was during this period that he was exposed to real wealth, through his friendship with one of his cousins. Jack's own family was solidly middle class; his cousin, on the other hand, lived in a mansion with a private swimming pool, multiple cars, a tennis court, huge bedrooms, fancy clothes, lots of pet dogs and even horses, and landscaping that made Jack think he was in heaven. Initially the boy was envious of his cousin, but he soon decided that someday he would create this same kind of abundant lifestyle for himself.

In the meantime, Jack held a number of part-time jobs, such as serving as a lifeguard at the local country-club pool. Although basically shy by nature, he was able to meet lots of pretty girls through his friends and go on double dates all over town. It wasn't long before he had his first girlfriend. His social life was so busy that he'd often forget to tell his stepdad and mom about his plans, and when he failed to come home on time, he would get grounded or have to do extra chores at home. But all things considered, it was a wonderful life for Jack.

The sound of the referee's whistle signaling the end of the High School City Championship Football Game marked the highlight of Jack's teenage years. He had just caught the winning touchdown pass seconds before and was heralded by his teammates as one of the heroes of the game. As Jack looked up in the stands and caught the eye of his girlfriend, he truly felt he was on top of the world, ready to take on whatever challenges might lie ahead.

Jack had never been at the top of his class in school, but he seemed always to be in the top three; in fact, he was in the top three in almost anything he did. When he was accepted to Harvard University, he was of course thrilled and proud, but he wasn't really surprised. He'd been told that Harvard had a policy to take two boys from West Virginia every year, and he knew that very few applied. Harvard seemed as foreign to most West Virginians as did Mars. For Jack, with his curiosity about the world, and his desire to always be in motion and discover new things, Harvard seemed ideal.

Jack had also been accepted at two of the nation's leading military service academies, the U.S. Naval Academy in Annapolis and the U.S. Army Military Academy at West Point. It was his mother's dream for him to attend Annapolis. Other family members thought West Point would be an even better choice. *His* feeling was that after eight years of military school, he already had a full appreciation for his family's military traditions, and it was time to explore new avenues. Jack thought long and hard about his decision, but in the end chose Harvard over Annapolis and West Point (not to mention Yale and Brown).

Jack still didn't remember anything about the Golden Motorcycle Gang or why he had decided to be born as a human being. However, he sensed that he was different from most of the people he'd grown up with in West Virginia. He didn't know what the difference was; for him it didn't need an explanation, it just *was,* and always had been, for as long as he could remember.

Jack had no trouble fitting in as he grew from a toddler to a boy to a man in West Virginia, but it always seemed as if he was looking for something different, expecting something more than his friends did.

He was hoping that he might find this "something more" in Cambridge, Massachusetts, while he attended Harvard.

Chapter 3

SOMETHING MORE

"And so, my fellow Americans, ask not
what your country can do for you; ask
what you can do for your country."

— JOHN F. KENNEDY

At first the "something more" Jack experienced at Harvard University was his beard. It was 1962, and the world was changing. John F. Kennedy was President of the United States, and he was asking young people like Jack to think "not what your country can do for you [but] what you could do for your country."

Hope for a better America and a better world was palpable, and for the first time in the country's history, it was the nation's youth who were leading the charge. To that end, 21-year-old Bob Dylan was singing

"Blowin' in the Wind" in the smoke- and hope-filled cafes along the Northeastern Seaboard of the United States.

However, not all winds were blowing for the better, as American involvement was rapidly escalating in the conflict in a remote Asian country few had ever heard of or could pronounce—a place called Vietnam.

When Jack arrived at Harvard, he gravitated to a Friday-night hootenanny group that sang traditional folk songs and, as Dylan and Joan Baez impacted the youth culture of the '60s, the group sang more and more peace and protest songs.

Jack's beard and increasingly long hair—which were partly the manifestation of a breaking away from the cropped haircuts and clean-shaven face required for his eight years of military school—fit in well with his new singing friends. Jack was only a freshman, so he thought the beard helped make him look older and more mature. The girls he met seemed to think the beard was pretty cool as well.

Initially Jack was singing for the fun of it and as a way to relax after a week of hitting the books. His classes at Harvard were much more challenging than those he had taken at the military school in West Virginia, and he found himself not only more intellectually involved in his studies, but emotionally invested as well.

Jack was finding that these folk-song-singing "peaceniks" (as many in the more skeptical older generation labeled those who pushed for peace and social progress through song and understanding) were making a lot of sense. The protest songs raised Jack's awareness about many social problems he'd never thought about in high school. His new friends would discuss and sing about the injustices caused by racism, sexism, and greed; along with the dangers of nuclear proliferation, overpopulation, the threats to clean air and water; and even the first rumblings of issues in a new movement just emerging called "environmentalism."

War in Vietnam seemed more and more inevitable, and although Jack retained a great respect for the military training he'd received at school in West Virginia, as well as for his family's tradition of service, he was beginning to doubt that war was really the right solution to international conflict. Jack understood the irony in his new skepticism, as he was grateful for the self-discipline he'd learned in military school and realized that the awakenings he was experiencing at Harvard wouldn't have been possible without this discipline.

Jack also knew that many of his friends from high school weren't waiting to be drafted and were volunteering to serve in Vietnam—and they were great kids dedicated to the American ideals of freedom, democracy, and the protection of those in need. Jack considered himself a true American patriot, but he also saw that keeping the peace should be the purpose of a military organization, rather than engaging in armed combat.

More than anything, Jack was dedicated to his studies, and was too busy with his heavy load of course work to make becoming a peace activist his primary focus. Originally drawn to courses about history and government because he thought he might someday become a lawyer, he decided to major in Chinese history.

On Friday, November 22, 1963, Jack was in New Haven, Connecticut, warming up for a football game between the Harvard and Yale intramural champions the day before the traditional Harvard–Yale game. But the game was cancelled 30 minutes before it was scheduled to start, due to the news that President John F. Kennedy had just been assassinated in Dallas.

Soon thereafter, the new President, Lyndon B. Johnson, was sworn in. He went on to institute the Great Society, a set of social programs focusing on civil rights and a more equitable distribution of opportunities for the underprivileged in America.

In the post-Kennedy era, Martin Luther King, Jr., emerged as the galvanizing force behind what would become known as the civil rights movement. Jack identified with King's "I Have a Dream" speech, and was inspired by him and other leaders of the movement to volunteer his services at an inner-city school near Cambridge. (It turned out to be an ideal situation in that this volunteer teaching opportunity also helped him qualify for an independent-study course, allowing him to receive university credit toward his undergraduate major.)

The more Jack was in close contact with the young African-American children at this school, most of whom came from poor or broken families, the more he realized how important it was to treat everyone with respect and kindness. As the child of divorce in a time when few middle-class parents separated, Jack saw himself in many of these boys and girls. He knew what it was like to be from a broken home; or to have a parent who might get drunk, angry, and behave violently or unpredictably. But Jack also knew that these kids had to deal with issues that were much worse than anything he'd ever experienced . . . and often on a daily basis to boot.

Speaking with these young kids, who were so alive and joyful at school but dealing with unimaginable challenges at home, made him think of Dale, an acquaintance he'd known back in Wheeling. Dale had been just plain mean. Although hunting was a way of life in Wheeling, Dale enjoyed torturing the animals he hunted before killing them. As he thought about his old acquaintance now, Jack realized that people, just like animals, could simply be in the wrong place at the wrong time and suffer the consequences.

Confronted with an opportunity to help now that he was student teaching, Jack wanted to do what he could to ensure that there would be fewer people creating "wrong place at the wrong time" situations. Jack decided that a career as a teacher in the inner city might be as effective a means of bringing a measure of peace to the world as the military career that his family had once intended for him.

MUSIC AND MAYHEM

"The important thing is not to stop questioning."

— ALBERT EINSTEIN

One of the pivotal moments in Jack's transformation from small-town boy from West Virginia to engaged world citizen occurred on July 25, 1965, at the Newport Folk Festival in Newport, Rhode Island. This happened to be the festival at which Bob Dylan used an electric guitar to play his folk songs for the first time. The folk-music purists in the audience were so against the use of these "nontraditional" guitars to sing "their music" that they actually booed Bob Dylan off the stage. Despite the amazing success he went on to enjoy in his career, he would wait 27 years before returning to perform again at the Newport Folk Festival.

However, the pivotal moment for Jack was not Dylan's bold choice—which signaled a change in the world of music that would impact millions of people for decades to come—but the opportunity, purely by accident, to sit next to Pete Seeger at a banjo performance the day before. For quite a while now, Jack had been singing songs originally performed by Peter, Paul and Mary; Woody Guthrie; and other great American folk singers, including Pete Seeger and his group the Weavers. To sit next to one of his idols, and to experience how genuine and approachable Seeger was, had a major impact on Jack. He realized that touching people through song was an amazing gift that allowed him to connect, and stay connected, to others in a way that his academic studies did not.

When Jack returned to Harvard in the fall of 1965 for his senior year, he resolved to take some courses that were more closely related to that passion for connecting to other people. His conversation with Pete Seeger—and his admiration for other musicians, including folk singer Donovan, groups such as the Lovin' Spoonful, and other musical acts singing about the important issues of the day—inspired Jack to take a course entitled Social Relations 10. That innocuous-sounding course changed Jack's life dramatically, exposing him to cutting-edge ideas in both sociology and psychology.

Many of the human potential movement's seminal thinkers and their theories were presented and discussed during Social Relations 10, and students were encouraged to experiment with many of these new ideas. For Jack, it was as though he had joined a human potential *encounter* group, where he was forced to examine his core beliefs at a level he had never before contemplated.

Although the revelations divulged sometimes made him feel uncomfortable, Jack found the exposure to this deeper level of self-examination compelling and almost addictive. For the first time, he realized the true power of ideas to alter his life and the lives of others. He decided that he wanted to explore these ideas further and focus not only on studying history, but on the field of educational psychology as well. At this point it was too late for Jack to change his major at Harvard, but he decided to pursue a career in public education anyway. He applied to, and was accepted for, graduate school at the University of Chicago to pursue a master's degree in education.

Some of Jack's classmates were surprised by his choice. His roommate even joked, "Well, when the rest of us are cashing in and enjoying the perks of our high-profile careers, we'll be sure to invite our buddy the public-high-school teacher to dinner."

Jack was not unaware of the financial advantages he might have had by leveraging his Harvard degree into a high-paying position in corporate America. But motivated by his encounter with Pete Seeger, along with his newly awakened awareness of the power of psychology to connect with and help others, he was at peace with the choice he'd made.

So, in the fall of 1966, Jack started graduate school. As a part of his training, he soon began visiting a wide range of Chicago-area public schools, including Rich Township High School, in what was in fact one of the richest suburbs of Chicago; and DuSable High School on the South Side of Chicago, in one of the poorest African-American neighborhoods in the city. (At the time, DuSable was actually considered the most dangerous high school in America.) The contrast between Rich Township and DuSable once again awakened Jack to the great inequalities in American society, with specific awareness of the challenges for teachers in underfunded and understaffed inner-city schools.

After completing his initial year of course work, Jack was assigned to spend a year teaching history at Calumet High School, also on the South Side of

Chicago. Calumet was an example of the rapidly shifting demographics occurring in the U.S. in the late 1960s. In fewer than five years, Calumet had transformed from a predominantly well-funded Jewish public school, to one that was poorly funded, with a nearly all-black student body.

At Calumet Jack was exposed directly to the scourge of teenage gangs and gang wars. Street gangs in high schools were not yet that common in American high schools in 1968, but Calumet did face this additional challenge.

One of the most tumultuous and impactful years in American history was just beginning, and Jack found himself at one of the epicenters of the country's violent struggle.

In 1968, both Martin Luther King, Jr., and Robert Kennedy were felled by assassins' bullets just two months apart. The anger and frustration felt by young people, already at a fever pitch because of resistance to the Vietnam War, ended up spilling into the streets of Chicago.

Yet Jack had already seen the city erupt in this way. The day after King had been shot, the grief and repressed rage boiled over to the point that Mayor Richard Daley ordered his police department to "shoot to kill" anybody suspected of committing arson, and President Johnson had to send state National Guard troops into the streets.

Violence begat violence.

As the situation spun further and further out of control, Jack realized that the status quo in American society was not really working; it had failed too many people, closing doors that needed to be opened wider to make progress possible for many. Jack was not radicalized, but for the first time he realized that his previous confidence in authority to make the right decisions, which was born of his strict upbringing and military education, might not be as well placed as he had previously believed.

Ironically, the roots of his emerging awareness—that is, of the value of not blindly following traditional authority—had been seeded by his disciplinarian father.

When Jack was six years old, he was involved in a car accident. Bud Canfield raced to the hospital when he learned what had happened and found his young son crying profusely. The injuries were minor, but the boy was distraught because all the other kids in his ward had been given ice cream as a late-afternoon snack, but he hadn't. And Jack loved ice cream.

After comforting his son, Bud found the head nurse, in her freshly starched white uniform, and asked why the boy hadn't been given any ice cream.

"The doctor was just getting ready to check on Jack, and we didn't think he should be eating ice cream before his checkup," she replied.

"I understand, but the checkup is over now. You're just keeping him here to wait for the test results tomorrow, so why can't he have some ice cream now?" Bud asked politely.

"Well, that just wouldn't be right. Snack time is over. Besides, we've already put the ice cream away, and the candy stripers who serve it have already gone home," the nurse explained, turning to go back to her desk at the front of the ward.

Bud grabbed her arm gently to get her attention and pleaded, "But, Nurse, my little boy has just had a major scare, and he feels it's not fair that he didn't get any ice cream when the other kids did. He sure would appreciate a dish right now."

"Rules are rules. I'm sorry, but there is nothing I can do," she said with an air of finality and walked away.

Jack looked sadly at his dad, but Bud just winked and told him, "Don't worry, son. I'll be back in a little bit, and you'll have your ice cream."

True to his word, within 30 minutes Bud had returned to Jack's bed with a five-gallon tub of ice cream, and enough plastic spoons and paper bowls for the entire children's ward of the hospital. Bud dished out a big bowl for his son, and then served the other young patients—all of whom felt a second bowl was just what they needed after dinner. The head nurse came barging down the aisle of beds and confronted Bud. "What are you doing with that?" she asked him loudly. "I told you, ice-cream time is over. This is against all hospital regulations!"

Unsure of what would happen next, Jack paused in the middle of swallowing a nice spoonful of the rich, creamy vanilla dessert. He was relieved when his father answered, in his most pleasant voice, "I know what you said about the rules and all, but some rules are just made to be broken. I don't see that Jack or any of the children here are going to be any the worse for having a bowl of ice cream. They all seem happy right now, and I doubt you'll have a peaceful evening if you take it away from them."

Although clearly irritated, the nurse just smoothed her uniform and muttered, "Well, I never . . ." and walked back to her nurse's station.

Jack continued eating, and the smile on his face was from much more than just the ice cream. He felt the strong love of his father and was proud of how his dad had stood up to the head nurse. Jack, being only six years old, had never really understood the bravery his dad had exhibited in flying B-17 bombers and in teaching others to fly planes—but that evening, he saw firsthand what he felt was great courage in Bud's defying the head nurse.

Jack remembered this incident during the raging fires of 1968, fires fanned by the authorities' intolerance and blind insistence on "order." He realized that if a strict and exacting person like Bud Canfield could see through the rules and get to a place of reason and fairness, his son could do no less.

Thus, when Jack saw the people on the South Side of Chicago standing up to the authority figures in their world, he committed himself to finding a way to help them and others who had been held down for too long by the economic and racial status quo in the U.S. Jack still respected the values of mainstream American society, but he saw the need for change in his country. And he was determined to contribute to correcting the severe inequalities he was observing.

Chapter 5

TALK TO ME

"Let us all hope that the dark clouds of racial prejudice will soon pass away and the deep fog of misunderstanding will be lifted from our fear-drenched communities and in some not too distant tomorrow the radiant stars of love and brotherhood will shine over our great nation with all of their scintillating beauty."

— MARTIN LUTHER KING, JR.

"Stop reading that book and talk to me."

Jack, who was doing his laundry, was startled by the intrusion of this dark-haired man he'd never met before. Since he was still in graduate school, Jack didn't have his own washing machine and had to frequent the local Laundromat. This particular Laundromat was located well within the mixed neighborhood of Italians, blacks, and other ethnic groups that made up Chicago's South Side. It was not a dangerous neighborhood, but for a young white man like Jack, it wasn't the safest place he had ever been either. So he was a little bit frightened at first when, out of the blue, his reading was interrupted by this rather strange request.

Jack was catching up on some reading for school while he waited for his clothes to dry, but he immediately put down his book and looked up.

"What did you say?" was his first response.

"You heard me. Stop reading your book and talk to me," the man repeated.

"Okay. What do you want to talk about?" Jack ventured cautiously, wanting to know if his questioner had a specific reason he wanted to talk.

"Well. Let's start with your name and why you're here. My name is Frank Broude, and I'm a doctoral student in economics, writing my dissertation on the best way to spend a federal-aid dollar to improve the city of Chicago."

"My name is Jack Canfield, and I'm a graduate student, too. I'm getting my master's degree in education and teaching at Calumet High School as part of my teacher training," Jack replied, beginning to feel more confident that he was dealing with a sane interloper

36

and not someone from whom he needed to protect himself.

And thus began one of the most important friendships in Jack's life. Frank Broude was an intense scholar who had a passion not just for economics, but for understanding how money could be used to make a difference in the lives of the disenfranchised.

For his dissertation, Frank was investigating how a dollar spent on education, or on a soup kitchen, or on hiring more police or firefighters, would impact the city. As he did his research, he couldn't help but focus on Chicago's greatest needs at the time. He found that they were primarily on the South Side of Chicago, thanks to the ghetto-like conditions being experienced by the city's African-American community.

Frank and Jack didn't just have an intellectual rapport when they started that first conversation in the Laundromat; they also had a shared interest in understanding the emotional and psychological components of Chicago's black community. As a teacher at Calumet High School, Jack was getting to know the lives of his students intimately. With Frank's support and passion for hands-on research inside the community (which was the focus of his dissertation), Jack started accompanying him to traditionally African-American restaurants, churches, and clubs. Frank was a great fan of jazz—and with Jack's interest and love for music, it didn't take long for him to become a fan of jazz as well.

Frank also took Jack to the primarily African-American church where Jesse Jackson was the reverend. Jack had never been that close to a speaker with the charisma of Jackson. He began to observe how Jackson captivated the entire room with his gestures and the tone of his voice, not just his words. Jack was inspired by Reverend Jackson—and oftentimes even more inspired by some of the speakers who would visit his church, such as comedian Bill Cosby and actor Sidney Poitier.

Jack was learning to greatly appreciate the African-American community and to champion the history and beauty of black culture.

At Calumet High School, Jack taught American history. It seemed ironic to him that although he was teaching black students, the official textbook for the course contained almost no mention of black Americans. Jack knew from his studies in educational psychology that self-esteem was a key element in getting students to focus on their studies. With very little mention of black history in the official textbook, he was going to have to find a way to connect his course to the lives of his students so that they would find meaning in what was for most of them just a collection of facts unrelated to their personal lives and interests.

In his search for some relevant history, Jack discovered a book by Lerone Bennett, Jr., entitled *Before the Mayflower: A History of the Negro in America 1619–1964,* and assigned it as ancillary reading for his students. The book chronicled the black experience in America from colonial times to the beginning of the civil rights movement in the early 1960s. Jack's students were captivated by this new information—so much so that they asked him if he would be the faculty sponsor for Calumet's newly forming African-American Student Organization. Jack accepted the role enthusiastically and was soon one of the few white teachers to be truly accepted and trusted by his black students.

This level of trust and respect proved to be of significant importance on April 5, 1968—the day after Dr. Martin Luther King, Jr., was killed.

Shortly after lunch on that Friday, the students at Calumet High School began to riot. They were running up and down the halls, completely out of control. They set wastebaskets on fire and threw desks out the windows. There was no immediate threat of violence, but the situation was volatile. Many of the white teachers shut themselves into the faculty-lounge area, and some of the students set off the fire alarm. When the Chicago Fire Department arrived, the firefighters were on high alert and ready to literally start bashing heads.

In the confusion of the crowded hallways, one of Jack's black students, who was also on the basketball team, accidentally bumped his towering 6'6" body into one of the large Irish-American firefighters. The student was pinned against the hall wall as the fireman, overcome with fear and anger, readied himself to strike the student on the side of the head with the blunt end of his ax.

Jack rushed to his student's rescue. Looking the fireman in the eye, he stated firmly, "You don't want to do that." The man eased off, and Jack later reflected that he'd perhaps saved his student's life that day just by being there and staying calm. He knew that his student wasn't intending to physically harm anyone—he was just letting out the intense feelings of frustration and hopelessness that King's assassination had brought to the surface in him, and in the entire black community.

During Jack's Calumet period, he also discovered what racism was truly about. He learned this in a way that surprised him, and it was more real than just reading about facts and figures and historical events.

Jack's best friend at the school was Claude Bossette, a tall black man who was a physical-education teacher. Claude and Jack organized Calumet's first swim team, and they'd spend not only part of their days together as coaches of the team, but many of their nights as well.

Claude would take Jack to all-black rib joints and clubs such as the Pumpkin Room, along with other businesses in which he'd be the only white person in the building. Jack had visited black jazz clubs and restaurants with Frank, but with Claude he was introduced to places even Frank didn't know about. Black patrons would look at Jack as he entered these eateries and clubs, and Claude would just say, "It's okay" or "He's with me." The questioning stares would quickly cease, and Jack would be accepted into these black-only establishments.

After many months of a very close friendship in which they often had conversations that would go into the wee hours of the morning, discussing the subjects most important to each of them on every level of their being, Jack felt he had a strong bond with Claude—and a true, lifelong best friend.

One morning, as Jack had his coffee in the faculty lounge at Calumet, Claude came up and told him, "I'm really sorry, but I can't be your friend anymore. Swimming season is over anyway, so it shouldn't be that awkward. Even so, I have to ask you not to approach me and ask me to dinner or to spend time with you after classes."

Jack was in shock. "Claude, we have such a great friendship," he said. "What's wrong?"

"Nothing's wrong. You know how passionate I am about my black roots and honoring my own heritage. Well, I joined the Black Muslim movement over the weekend, and my black brothers feel it's inappropriate for me to continue to associate with white people. It's not personal, but being true to my black heritage and my new religion is more important to me than our friendship," Claude explained clearly and without emotion.

"This makes no sense to me," was all Jack could say.

"It does to me," was his friend's reply. Then he stood up and walked out of Jack's life forever.

Jack was stunned. He thought he understood racism and was above being racist in his personal life. He thought he understood what it meant to be discriminated against. But it was only when Claude discriminated against him simply because he was white that

Jack absolutely "got" on an emotional level what discrimination felt like. Intellectually he could see why Claude felt the need to do what he did, but emotionally he felt betrayed and outraged. He was still Jack. He had not changed in any way. Why was his best friend cutting him out of his life just because he had white skin?

The lesson Jack learned in that moment was subtle and painful but also important. He realized to a degree he never had before how devastating intolerance of any kind can be. In later years he'd have an acute sense of how the feeling of separation—no matter how well intended—could hurt and destroy relationships. Ultimately this lesson would become a valuable asset on his path toward fulfilling his purpose as a member of the Golden Motorcycle Gang.

Chapter
6

THE STONE FOUNDATION

"Everyone has inside himself a piece of good news!
The good news is that you really don't know how
great you can be, how much you can love, what you
can accomplish, and what your potential is!"

— ANNE FRANK

In life, one minor decision sometimes leads to events that could not possibly be anticipated. Jack's decision to befriend Frank Broude at the Laundromat on Blackstone Avenue on the South Side of Chicago, for instance, created a series of events that unknowingly brought him ever closer to his destiny of reuniting the Golden Motorcycle Gang.

Early in their friendship, Frank told Jack about a lecture series that he was attending at Kendall College in nearby Evanston. Called the Living Philosopher Series, the speakers included people such as Marshall McLuhan, who taught that "the medium is the message"; Alan Watts, who spoke about the mystical powers of Zen meditation; Constantinos Doxiadis, a Greek architect and city planner who was an expert on the human element in architecture; and famed family therapist Virginia Satir, among others.

One of the talks that most impacted Jack was given by Dr. Herbert Otto. As the director of the National Center for the Exploration of Human Potential in Los Angeles, Dr. Otto was already known in the late 1960s as one of the fathers of the human potential movement. His lecture at Kendall addressed his belief that human beings only use 10 percent of their mental potential; then he gave examples of how, in the right circumstances, people could learn five or more foreign languages, develop superior mathematical and scientific skills, and uncover other abilities thought to be superhuman by most educators.

Jack was mesmerized by the talk and approached Dr. Otto afterward. "I'm fascinated by your work, and only wish I lived in California so that I could learn more about your research," he confessed.

"Well, I know your studies require you to stay here in Chicago, but you might consider attending some of the workshops put on by the Oasis Center here. Oasis is dedicated to providing seminars and workshops focusing on the full development of human potential, and it's funded by insurance mogul W. Clement Stone through his foundation," Dr. Otto explained.

"Well, if you recommend that I attend these workshops, I'll sign up immediately," Jack enthusiastically replied.

"Good. We all owe a great debt to Clement Stone. With the resources provided by his foundation, Oasis is bringing in some of the foremost thinkers and group leaders from every field in psychology and human development. You will not regret your decision." And, of course, Dr. Otto was correct. Jack never regretted one minute he spent at the Oasis workshops, and he attended almost every weekend for a year. He was exposed to every type of psychological practitioner, from self-hypnosis experts to those working in the new field of humanistic psychology—not to mention encounter group specialists, Gestalt therapists, and speakers fresh from the Esalen Institute. (Esalen was and is a retreat center located in Big Sur, California. There, those in charge develop new approaches to therapy, motivation, and learning.) It was a very exciting time . . .

and more opportunities to learn and grow were just around the corner.

In June 1968, Jack was offered a full-time position with the Job Corps Center in Clinton, Iowa. Although the job only paid $8,000 a year, Jack didn't hesitate to take it. Administered by the U.S. Department of Labor, Job Corps was an educational- and vocational-training program that aimed to help young people improve the quality of their lives. Jack had been offered the job based largely on his teaching experience in Chicago, where he had developed a keen practical understanding of the challenges of teaching economically and culturally disadvantaged students.

Jack understood that these kids needed more than just assignments and individual attention from teachers a few minutes a day. He realized that if a program could be created that would be both interactive and under the student's personal control, that student would become more involved and engaged and would progress much faster. So he jumped into his new educational project with limitless enthusiasm and energy.

As part of his job, Jack met with consultants from all parts of the world, who traveled to the converted

Veterans Administration Hospital in Iowa where he was now based. Jack and his colleagues ultimately came to feel that they were making real progress, which would eventually lead to individualized learning programs for inner-city children with reading difficulties. Nevertheless, the Job Corps assignment was challenging, to say the least. The immediate task was to take students from underprivileged backgrounds who had dropped out of, or been expelled from, school, and bring them to an educational level where they would be employable. The student population mostly consisted of black, Hispanic, Native-American, and mixed-race young women . . . and all of them faced significant challenges. Many of them had dropped out of school because they'd gotten pregnant. Others had gotten into trouble with the law. Still others had just failed their classes. And the majority of them had gone to very poor-quality schools and been treated as second-class citizens.

The students were housed on the second floor of a two-story building in Clinton, Iowa. Quite a few of them had grown up on reservations in South Dakota— they'd never been on the second story of a building in their lives, and the only African Americans they had ever seen were portrayed as criminals on television shows. With the mixture of cultures, and a white teacher from West Virginia, it was a true case of "culture shock" for these students.

But Jack was young and motivated and full of energy. Part of his assignment was not just to teach, but to help create the new curriculum as well. He knew that many of the female students were hoping to become nurses or qualify for additional professional training. Qualification for such programs required a minimum of a tenth-grade reading level; unfortunately, on average, students came to this Jobs Corps facility with a *fourth*-grade reading level. By developing a highly innovative reading program, Jack and his colleagues created a way to raise the students' reading levels, and a great deal of them were able to qualify for the next levels of vocational and professional training available through additional programs.

While living in rural Clinton, Jack also started dating a beautiful young African-American woman who taught at the Jobs Corps Center as well. Clinton didn't have much of a black population, except at Job Corps; and in 1968, it was still unusual to see a mixed-race couple, especially in small-town America. To escape the constant stares and take advantage of the entertainment and cultural opportunities that did not exist in Clinton, Jack and his girlfriend would often make the relatively short drive to Chicago on the weekends.

One of those weekends was during the 1968 Democratic National Convention. During that time, there were speeches by anti–Vietnam War presidential candidate and activist Eugene McCarthy, as well as gatherings and protest marches attended by scores of young people. Jack and his girlfriend actually participated in one of these marches; however, since they needed to get back to Clinton that evening, they had to leave a rally they were attending at about 5 P.M.

As they were driving, the radio began airing bulletins about the riots and police action that had started just after they'd left the city. Jack had noticed the large number of police—all of whom seemed to be six feet tall or taller, with scowling faces as they "kept order" and prevented the protesters from getting "out of control"—but he didn't know what had happened to incite the "riot" and subsequent reports of police brutality. After returning to Clinton, he watched news clips on TV, and among those being "controlled by the police" with batons and harsh beatings were several friends whom he knew were among the most peaceful and loving people he had ever met.

Although Jack's father had been in the Air Force, and his stepfather was a naval officer, he did not believe in continuing the war in Vietnam. He had joined several protests to advocate the position even many military leaders were starting to voice: that America needed to end this war as quickly as possible. That stance was all these demonstrators in Chicago had been voicing as well. Jack was shocked that Mayor Daley had used the police to crush those who were openly opposing what they felt were misguided policies. The protestors were acting not as traitors, but as loyal believers in the principles of American democracy—including freedom of speech.

Just as Jack was beginning to be radicalized by these and similar experiences, his Job Corps experience came to an abrupt end. As a result of Richard Nixon's election in November, there was a change in federal funding—the Job Corps program in which he was teaching was moved to another city several hundreds of miles away, in a Republican congressman's district. Jack's position was eliminated during the move, so he was out of a job.

It was a blessing that Jack had developed contact with the W. Clement & Jessie V. Stone Foundation in Chicago through the workshops he'd attended at Oasis. Thanks to that connection, and his inner-city teaching experience, he was offered a position by the

Stone Foundation in June 1969. When the president of the Foundation offered Jack the job—in which he would conduct teacher trainings on how to motivate students to want to learn and achieve—he told him that while Jack was employed, he could continue to attend any workshops or teacher training that he chose. Jack was elated and took full advantage of the opportunities he was given, attending almost 20 trainings in his first year of employment alone.

One of the synchronicities of Jack's position was that his office was in the same building as the offices of W. Clement Stone's *Success* magazine. The managing editor of the magazine at the time was Og Mandino, who was famous for writing some of the best-selling books on salesmanship ever published. He was focused on helping salespeople, corporate managers, and entrepreneurs become more successful. Jack was focused on helping underprivileged children overcome the disadvantages they faced, and become more successful as well. While the target audiences were different, the principles and techniques were the same.

By this time, Jack had become a liberal Democrat, focused on creating equal opportunities for all Americans. Og Mandino and Clement Stone, on the other hand, were major supporters of the Republican

Party—and part of what Jack viewed as the conservative business class that controlled America.

Jack was confused by how Clement Stone, a member of the wealthy conservative elite of America, could fund and support his own work with the poorest, most challenged members of American society. He'd occasionally see Mr. Stone visiting with Og Mandino and other executives of the magazine in the building. So when he found himself alone in a meeting with the man, he felt compelled to say, "Mr. Stone, I greatly appreciate the opportunity you've given me. But sometimes I wonder how you can be so interested in funding the education of people who have a radically different view from you in terms of their own politics and aspirations. I don't want to offend you, but how do you reconcile your staunch Republican and conservative principles with having a liberal like me working for you?"

Mr. Stone chuckled and explained, "When working with people, the key is to focus on where your interests and goals overlap, not where they differ." Then he drew this diagram on a piece of paper:

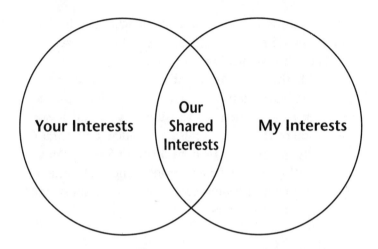

"Like you, I believe that it is essential for the growth and well-being of this great country that we educate all Americans," he continued. "The kids in the inner city are going to be better Americans if they're well educated. I want them to learn to take 100 percent responsibility for their lives, eliminate the word *can't* from their vocabulary, identify their strengths, set goals, and take action. I want them to believe in their dreams—believe that they can achieve anything they want to—and never give up.

"From what I know of you, Jack, you also want these things. So let's spend our time focusing on where our goals overlap and what we can do together, rather than focusing on or arguing about what we disagree on. If you do that in life, you'll get a lot more accomplished with people. I know I have."

With that, Mr. Stone got up, shook Jack's hand, and exited the room.

Jack realized that he'd just had a special lesson from one of the greatest business leaders and philanthropists in America. He'd go on to have many more conversations with Clement Stone—and each time he learned powerful lessons from these often short, but always rich, encounters.

After a little more than a year of wonderful challenges and successes at the Stone Foundation, Jack decided he'd learned all he could from his time there, and that it was time to continue his formal education. He applied to, and was accepted into, the doctoral program in psychological education at the University of Massachusetts Amherst. Soon he would be learning and perfecting more tools, and deepening the wisdom that would allow him to reconnect with the Golden Motorcycle Gang.

THE LIGHTS IN MASSACHUSETTS

"If you do follow your bliss you put yourself on a kind of track that has been there all the while, waiting for you, and the life that you ought to be living is the one you are living. . . . Wherever you are—if you are following your bliss, you are enjoying that refreshment, that life within you, all the time."

— JOSEPH CAMPBELL

Now in his mid-20s, Jack was ready to move back to a rural setting. He had loved Chicago, but at heart he was a small-town boy who yearned to be closer to nature, surrounded by trees and animals and a slower pace of life. At UMass he was able to enjoy the bucolic lifestyle of Amherst, surrounded by a high level of intellectual activity and self-development that he now required to feel totally alive and creative. Many of his friends from Harvard (including some of his "peacenik" hootenanny friends) lived in the area, and he had the best of both worlds in terms of what he valued, both in nature and in culture.

Jack enjoyed his classes and was particularly taken with one on educational motivation. In fact, it was during this class that he experienced one of the pivotal moments of his life.

The professor asked students about their own motivations to teach. "Think back to the first moment you realized that this was what you wanted," he instructed. "Feel that moment and write down how it changed your life and prompted you to become a teacher."

The other students responded in conventional ways, but not Jack. He found himself writing about a feeling he had of being a spiritual being riding through the universe with other spiritual beings on golden motorcycles. He was in a joyous state and marveling at the miracle of creation when his attention was drawn to a small blue planet. His first thought was that this planet was in trouble. He wasn't sure why it was in trouble or if he could help, but he had an instant sense that he should go down and investigate.

As Jack focused his attention on the small blue sphere, he recognized that ignorance was at the core of the problems on the planet at that time. The majority of human beings had restricted and limited views of the true nature of reality. They were caught in beliefs that there weren't enough resources for everyone, and that life on planet Earth was a zero-sum game in which the success of one individual or group came at the expense of other individuals or groups. As a cosmic being, Jack knew this was incorrect thinking.

It was in that moment of visualizing himself as a golden motorcyclist that Jack realized that his desire to be a teacher was a spiritual as well as a vocational calling. He snapped out of his reverie and turned in his assignment. His professor told him that he had a "great imagination." Neither of them thought much more about it—it had just been a vision, a daydream. Interesting, yes, but not a vision around which Jack could create an actual teaching career. Or was it?

Jack dedicated himself to his studies with even greater energy and enthusiasm than before. He was becoming a leader in his field—other students were fascinated by his ideas about using "guided imagery" and cutting-edge psychological techniques to revolutionize learning, and so were his professors. He explained to all of them how his research and techniques were valuable not just for teaching inner-city children, but for *all* children everywhere (and adults, too).

Jack most keenly focused on what he believed was the most critical component enabling children to learn: self-esteem. Thanks to everything he'd been taught over the years, both in school and on the job, he'd found that children lacking this essential trait were too insecure to take chances and potentially fail or embarrass themselves. Instead, they tended to avoid class altogether or take the damaging position that the schoolwork didn't matter in the "real world." Jack had determined that many of these dysfunctional postures and reactions among inner-city kids were masking low self-esteem.

He reasoned that it's largely impossible for children to learn in an environment in which they're both highly uncomfortable and failing to recognize the value, to themselves and their futures, of what they're being taught. Teaching children to have self-worth, not just inside the classroom, but in terms of their motivation to learn on the whole, would be of the utmost benefit to them.

Jack's keen recognition of the social dynamics at work inside of a classroom (and of a school on the whole) helped him understand that learning, like any trend, can become contagious among students. Greater self-esteem and learning capacity among his most challenged students would function as a "rising tide" and lift up all of his students, even those who didn't exhibit motivational deficiencies.

He started to do the research for his doctoral thesis on the topic of student self-concept and academic achievement. Yet he recognized that the information was so immediately needed by teachers that he collected his findings into his first published book, *100 Ways to Enhance Self-Concept in the Classroom,* which he co-authored with Dr. Harold Clive Wells.

Despite the academic-sounding title, the book did extremely well—selling more than 400,000 copies to a diverse group of readers. For the first time in his life, Jack had some extra spending money.

More important, though, the book generated demand from his many readers for his services as a consultant and a teacher trainer. He was delighted to spend more and more time teaching and consulting, and was enjoying the material benefits of being paid three to four times more per hour as a consultant than he had ever been paid working for Job Corps or the Stone Foundation.

It was through his ongoing research for his consulting work that he met a young psychologist named Judy who had studied with Fritz Perls, the originator of Gestalt therapy. Jack began to expand his own studies to include Gestalt therapy—and before he knew it, he and Judy had fallen in love.

Judy was full of energy and idealism and believed that Jack was one of the most brilliant men she had ever met. She encouraged him to expand his consulting practice; as he became more focused on doing so, he was less motivated to complete the final requirements for his Ph.D.

Jack had taken to heart one of the lessons that he had learned directly from W. Clement Stone. He vividly remembered the conversation in which Mr. Stone had asked him if he took 100 percent responsibility for his life. Jack's response at the time had been, "I think so."

"This is a yes or no question, young man. You either do or you don't."

"Well, I guess I'm not sure."

"Have you ever blamed anyone for the circumstances in your life? Have you every complained about anything?"

"Uh . . . yeah . . . I guess I have."

"Don't guess. Think."

"Yes, I have."

"Okay, then. That means you don't take responsibility for your life. True success in life will only come when you take *100 percent responsibility* for your life, and realize that you both created the circumstances for your past and present and have the ability to create the circumstances for your future. Do you understand that?"

"Yes, sir, I do."

Jack firmly believed that he could create the circumstances to have a wonderful life with Judy by his side. In May 1972 they married, and he took a leave of absence from his doctoral program. Jack was becoming firmly established as a leader in his field, and he didn't see the need for the official approval and acknowledgment that the doctoral degree conferred to continue his consulting.

Judy was supportive of Jack's decision, and although she wasn't from a wealthy family, she did have a small trust fund that allowed them to establish a retreat center where the two of them could continue their consulting. They called it the New England Center for Personal and Organizational Development, and while Judy conducted Gestalt-therapy groups, Jack focused on instructing teachers and others on the techniques he had originally presented in *100 Ways to Enhance Self-Concept in the Classroom.*

Visitors came to the center from all over the country, and Jack was able to continue to do research and expand his own exploration into all aspects of psychology. Before long, he and Judy also had two children, Oran and Kyle. For more than five years, the New England Center allowed Jack the freedom to be both a dad and a breadwinner. However, he eventually felt the desire to reach more people . . . and he and Judy also came to realize that they were not well suited for a lifetime of marriage together.

Jack had begun to understand that his success so far, and his vision for what lay ahead, relied so much on connecting with the right people at the right moment—a synchronicity of paths. He also realized that it was necessary at times to disconnect, however painfully, from those whose paths diverged from his own. He took full responsibility for the unhappiness that was part of his life with Judy, and the two of them divorced in 1977.

Jack began to consider what he should do next. He had always paid attention to the signs he received from the workshops he attended as part of his ongoing research and education. At one of them, which was conducted by Jean Houston in upstate New York, Jack and the other participants were directed to create a new language. Then, without thinking, they were to write a poem in that language and then translate it into English as fast as possible. When the group was asked to read their poems out loud, most of them were simple and delicate. In Jack's case, his poem was neither. It was more like a great epic, about a general leading his massive army across the Russian steppe on the way to a large conquest. Even Jack was somewhat taken aback by the grand scale of his poem.

In another exercise, the participants were asked to swallow a small piece of dirt and then imagine what might grow forth from it. Again, almost everyone in the group imagined delicate flowers or modest leaves emerging, but not Jack. He imagined the growth of a bamboo forest that quickly populated the entire world and then spread its roots out to the moon.

He became concerned that there might be an ego-maniacal aspect to his visions, but when he shared his feelings with Jean, she told him not to worry. "It is not megalomania that causes you to have such big

65

visions," she told him. "It is the reality that unlike many of the other people here, you do, in fact, have a huge destiny ahead of you. Your work, whatever it is, is intended to reach every corner of the globe."

This feedback reassured Jack, but it also made him rethink his choices in keeping his small New England Center as his primary focus, and as a way to reach "every corner of the globe."

Jack was going through many changes in his life. In 1978, he remarried a wonderful woman named Georgia who supported his desire to reach more people and face new challenges. Within a few years, Jack realized he needed to sell or shut down the center and position himself so that he could reach a larger group of teachers and leaders.

He wasn't exactly sure what he would do next . . . but when he was offered a position in California, he sold his Massachusetts property, shut down the center with Georgia's assistance, and moved ever closer to fulfilling his destiny.

Chapter 8

CALIFORNIA DREAMING

"Meditation gives you an opportunity to come to know your invisible self. It allows you to empty yourself of the endless hyperactivity of your mind, and to attain a calmness. It teaches you to be peaceful, to remove stress, to receive answers where confusion previously reigned. . . ."

— DR. WAYNE W. DYER

The year was 1984, and California was the place to be. Apple Computer, Hewlett-Packard, Intel, and other successful companies were bringing additional high-tech industries to Silicon Valley and transforming the state. The economy was booming, and opportunities were emerging everywhere.

Jack joined Insight Training Seminars, based near the beach in Santa Monica (on the western edge of Los Angeles). He was now leading training seminars for hundreds of people a week, not just 20 or 30 as he had with his own small center in Massachusetts. In addition, he was traveling all over the United States to give self-esteem workshops. St. Louis, Philadelphia, Miami, Boston, San Diego, San Francisco, and Washington, D.C., were all part of the regular circuit of workshops organized by Insight.

He was also being introduced to many of the people at the cutting edge of the human potential movement. Along with John-Roger, the founder of Insight, Jack met Werner Erhard, the founder of est; pioneering psychotherapist Dr. Carl Rogers; psychologist Will Schutz; and best-selling self-help authors Peter McWilliams, Dr. Gerald Jampolsky, Dr. Barbara De Angelis; and Dr. John Gray, among many others.

Jack also met Marilyn Ferguson, whose book *The Aquarian Conspiracy* went to the number one position on the *New York Times* bestsellers list and signaled that New Age and California trends were now mainstream for the entire country, as they soon would be for the world.

Jack was flourishing. He realized that he could make a true difference in people's lives when he spoke to them about generating greater self-esteem, both for their students and colleagues and for themselves.

As he became more successful, he had more opportunities to meet with some of the less visible but vital thinkers behind the human potential movement. Jack recognized a new element of spiritual awakening emerging as he began to get in touch with his sense of purpose and his personal destiny. He was starting to feel increasingly connected to humanity as a whole, but it was still an indistinct type of connection.

That lack of clarity changed on the fateful day he visited Stewart Emery.

Stewart Emery was a pioneer in his teachings. Jack had taken his Actualization Training several years before in Boston, finding it to be more powerful than any of the other human potential programs he had explored up to that point. Now he arranged to meet privately with Stewart in his office in Tiburon, California, just over the Golden Gate Bridge from downtown San Francisco.

Jack had purposefully scheduled the appointment at this moment in his professional and personal development. He now believed that he would most greatly benefit from Stewart's keen and practical insights into how to unleash his clients' potential—to take positive action to produce personal, organizational, and social change that had a lasting impact.

When he arrived for his appointment, he was told to take a seat in Stewart's private office. Jack had never been in such a Zen space before. He sat in front of a desk that had absolutely nothing on it, not even a telephone. Behind the desk was a credenza that was completely empty, except for a phone, and on the wall was an imposing painting of a lion.

Stewart walked in a few minutes later, shook Jack's hand, and took his seat behind the desk. As he sat down, he smiled and asked, "What can I do for you?"

Jack made eye contact with Stewart but found he could not speak.

He looked away and then looked back at Stewart. He still couldn't speak.

He looked away again and then locked Stewart in an eye-to-eye silence that lasted for what seemed to him to be several very long minutes.

Jack didn't know what was happening.

Stewart just smiled softly and maintained eye contact until Jack finally was able to utter, "I don't understand what is happening, but I can barely speak. It's as if all of space has expanded, but I can't form thoughts . . . I'm merely receiving images and ideas in an endless stream."

"Well that *is* what is happening," explained Stewart. "Right now at this time in my life, I am holding a very high level of consciousness. As you sit there, your consciousness is responding to the space I'm holding.

"My work in the last few years has been about holding and creating space for my students and clients to experience and expand into their own higher consciousness. Once you expand into that, you will be able to speak. Just take your time. We can talk, or not, as you feel moved."

Eventually, Jack was able to focus on the images and thoughts he was receiving, and he began sharing these with Stewart.

"You are exceptional in being able to access what I have to teach so quickly," Stewart replied with his unique calm and sense of inner knowing.

Jack was never the same from that moment forward. Thereafter, his work reflected the greater spiritual awareness he felt in all that he did.

Jack and Stewart remained in contact for many years, and it was through their discussions that Jack began to remember both the euphoria of riding his golden motorcycle throughout the universe, along with the reason he had incarnated as a human being.

As Jack meditated more and more regularly, his consciousness began to expand even further. During one meditation, he saw Stewart on a silver motorcycle, riding with his own gang of friends.

When he asked Stewart about the image he'd received of the silver motorcyclists, his friend winked and told him, "Yes, my generation was the Silver Motorcycle Gang. We were told that we were to hold the space until the Golden Motorcycle Gang was ready. You are the first to arrive, and I am here to help you, as are the rest of the Silver Motorcycle Gang. You should understand that not all of the Silver Motorcycle Gang even knows that they're part of it, but they will be able to help you nonetheless."

Giving Jack a big smile, Stewart said, "It's good that you have finally realized who you really are. There is a lot of work to be done."

FROM SILVER TO GOLD

"God made man because he loves stories."

— ELIE WIESEL

Shortly after Jack's extraordinary "conversation" with Stewart, strange coincidences and synchronicities began to occur.

He would be on an airplane bound for a training session, and the person sitting next to him would somehow be connected with his work or his life purpose. He would be attending a professional conference, and others would unexpectedly ask him to join them for lunch. Some of these "chance encounters" were with people older than Jack who had much wisdom to impart. In several instances, he was almost certain that they were members of Stewart's Silver Motorcycle Gang, but he never felt bold enough to ask.

In truth, the concept of Golden and Silver Motorcycle Gangs still seemed a little implausible to Jack, except for those times when he was surrounded by the mystical aura of his meditations, or when he was in dialogue with Stewart.

Jack had the opportunity through his work and travels to spend more and more time with leading thinkers and scientists such as John C. Lilly, who was a pioneer in the field of communication with dolphins. Jack was immediately drawn to Lilly's work, and to the principle that animals are intelligent and deserving of human respect. He had long felt a sense of not wanting to hurt other living creatures. In all his endeavors, even as a young man in athletics, Jack had prided himself on his ability to win at games or achieve objectives not by hurting others or using force, but through the use of physical agility and the outsmarting of his opponents.

Although Jack was enjoying wonderful success as an Insight trainer, he had an inner sense that he was meant to do more. So when he wasn't giving trainings himself, he was going to as many workshops for his own development as he could.

One of the workshops he attended was taught by John Gray (who would later write *Men Are from Mars, Women Are from Venus*) and Barbara De Angelis, and it included an exercise called the "Total Truth process." It was during this exercise that Jack realized the truth of his own situation: he really wanted to have his own training company and not just be a trainer for Insight. He felt comfortable teaching and facilitating the seven different workshops he conducted for the company, but only two of the seven were based on curricula that he had developed or co-developed himself. He wanted the challenge and reward of teaching his own material, and of being able to experiment and push the boundaries of what he was presenting. He wanted to be the captain of his own ship once again.

Empowered by the workshop—as well as by his new level of comfort with seeking his own inner voice, which he had learned from Stewart—Jack made the decision to leave Insight and start his own training company. He had to borrow $10,000 from his mother-in-law to get started, but he made the commitment to be profitable in his first month of business . . . because if he wasn't, he would be out of business.

Jack still saw himself as a kid from a small town in West Virginia, and it wasn't until experiencing the Total Truth process that he was able to admit to himself that in reality, only fear had been holding him back. He knew that he could teach groups of hundreds of people successfully, but he hadn't felt ready to take his shot at his true dream: to run his own large group-training program.

Only when Jack realized that he was willing to let go of the security and acclaim he was receiving as an Insight trainer was he able to transition to his true dream of doing not just what he wanted, but *exactly* what he wanted. He recognized the truth that it was only his fear of the business dynamics of running a large training company that was holding him back. Once he let go of that fear, he soared like an eagle.

Jack's career immediately went into high gear. His annual salary jumped from $38,000 a year to more than $140,000 annually. He realized that he no longer needed to focus on meeting only his basic needs—he was ready to continue the inner work he had learned from Stewart and others and pursue his larger life purpose.

As Jack's career evolved, he started to meet people around his own age (he was now in his late 30s) whom he could sense were part of his mission. One of these people was a gentleman named Mark Victor Hansen, whom Jack had met in the mid-1980s.

Mark was a motivational speaker and entrepreneur intent on helping others flourish personally and professionally. He'd studied for many years with Buckminster Fuller, so he'd learned of the amazing potential of human beings that "Bucky" always mentioned in his talks. Mark lived in this world of ideas and was always finding ways to help others take their work, or their visions, and make them bigger and more powerful.

During a breakfast in 1991, Jack shared with Mark that he was working on compiling a book of true stories that would inspire people to be all they could be in every area of their lives. Jack had been using the stories to teach the principles of love, forgiveness, acceptance, goal setting, taking action, and perseverance as part of the Self-Esteem and Peak Performance workshops he was conducting.

Invariably, the attending students would come up to him afterward (in some cases, many weeks afterward) to tell him how memorable and inspirational a particular story had been for them. They also kept asking if he planned to put these stories into a book that they could buy. These attendees wanted to be able to share Jack's stories with their children, employees, and church groups.

After six or seven people in less than a week asked him about the possibility of a book, Jack realized he really did need to put something together. He'd gone on to collect about 70 stories and was ready to approach book publishers with a proposal.

When Mark heard about Jack's idea, he thought it was fantastic. It turns out that he also used similar stories in many of the speeches he gave. He said, "Jack, I love your concept, and I would be happy to contribute another 30 or so. That way, the book would then have 101 stories. When I was in graduate school, I spent a year studying and working in India, where I learned that '101 is the number of completion.' So, I think that would be the ideal number for the book. Would you be willing to consider having me as a co-author?"

Jack thought about it for a few minutes and then realized that with Mark's enthusiasm and assistance, the book could only become better—and with Mark's expertise in marketing and sales, it would ultimately reach more people. "Okay, that sounds great," he replied. "I'll send you my stories to read and you send me yours, and we'll get this completed as soon as possible."

"As soon as possible" in the book-publishing business is often a period of about two years. While it didn't take that long for Jack and Mark to complete their book, it *did* take almost two years to find a publisher willing to invest in the project.

Of course, the right people are always worth the wait. . . .

Chapter 10

AN AMAZING DREAM

"Fall seven times, stand up eight."

— JAPANESE PROVERB

Jack and Mark had no trouble coming up with 101 stories for their book, but they did struggle somewhat with finding a title.

Since meeting with Stewart Emery, Jack had been practicing meditation and yoga every morning, and he'd learned to trust the ideas that came to him. So he decided that he would spend every morning for a full week in meditation, thinking up just the perfect title for his stories. Mark committed to do the same.

For the first three days, no great title came to either of them. On the fourth morning, however, Jack awoke from a vivid dream. In it he had seen a large green chalkboard, similar to those he'd used in classrooms as a schoolteacher. While looking at the chalkboard, he had seen a large hand write the words *chicken soup,* in large yellow letters.

At first Jack didn't know what to think. *What does chicken soup have to do with our book?* he wondered.

A voice, which he thought of as God's, responded, "When you were a child, your grandmother gave you chicken soup when you were sick."

"But this isn't a book about sick people," he replied.

"Oh yes, it is," the voice insisted. "People's spirits are sick. They are frightened and resigned to leading lives of quiet desperation. Your book will help lift and heal people's spirits. You are providing medicine that will heal their souls."

Jack immediately had goose bumps, as he realized that *Chicken Soup for the Soul* was, in fact, the perfect title for his book. He woke up his wife, Georgia, and told her the title. She also got goose bumps, and confirmed, "That is the perfect title for your book."

Jack called Mark, who had instant goose bumps, too. They called their literary agent, Jeff Herman, and even *he* got goose bumps. They were all certain that they had found the ideal title. They worked together to create the subtitle *101 Stories to Open the Heart and Rekindle the Spirit,* and off went the book proposal to the leading publishing houses.

Apparently, none of the editors at any of the 40 publishing houses to whom the book proposal was originally submitted got goose bumps, though—they all turned the project down. Jeff told Jack and Mark that he had no more publishers to solicit, and they began to resign themselves to self-publishing.

The year was 1992, and the practice of writers publishing their own books was neither easy nor common. Jack was still researching the best company to work with to produce this collection of stories when a friend mentioned to him that the American Booksellers Association would be holding their annual convention in Anaheim, California, and authors could purchase floor passes to visit the more than 400 publishers that would be exhibiting there.

Mark and Jack discussed it, and thought it would be worth investigating whether they could connect directly with a publisher or editor during the show. They printed up a few dozen spiral-bound samples of the best 30 stories from their book, put them in a backpack, and walked the floor of the Anaheim Convention Center. Yet even with face-to-face meetings, they couldn't get many editors to accept copies of their sample. They were told that compilations of stories didn't sell, especially from authors who were relatively unknown to booksellers and the general public.

On the last day of the conference Jack saw the booth of Health Communications, Inc. (HCI), a small publisher based in Deerfield Beach, Florida. The owner of the company, Peter Vegso, had met Jack several years earlier while attending one of Jack's self-esteem conferences. Peter now greeted Jack, and after a few pleasantries, Jack presented him with a copy of his sample book.

"Normally I wouldn't read this," Peter told him, looking directly in his eyes. "However, I know you, and I know how people respond to you when you speak—so let me have my partner, Gary Seidler, read it and see what he thinks. The reality is that our core business of recovery books has been soft for the last year or so, and we need to find some new types of books to publish."

Jack and Mark got together when the conference ended. Since only HCI had shown any interest at all, the two of them completed their research on which companies to work with to help them produce their book. Yet a week after the conference, much to Jack's surprise—and fortunately before Mark had made any final commitment to the printer—Peter called, full of enthusiasm.

"I didn't expect Gary to like your book, but he just came back from the beach where he goes to read new manuscripts, and he told me he cried while reading it," he said. "He loves the stories and wants us to offer you a contract. I read a few of the stories myself and can see why he was so moved."

"That's great! Go ahead and send over the contract, and Mark and I will make a decision quickly," Jack replied, ecstatic that a publisher had finally recognized the power of his book.

When the contract arrived, Jack and Mark were disappointed that there was no advance. They also learned that the initial print run would only be 5,000 copies. When they pressed for a larger printing, explaining how they were going to be going all over the country promoting the book, Peter wouldn't budge. It was only after Mark and Jack guaranteed that they would purchase any unsold copies that HCI upped the first printing to 20,000 copies.

It took a lot of hard work, but after 14 months of constant promotion—with as many as five interviews a day—the book landed on *The Washington Post* best-sellers list, and found a spot on *The New York Times* list two weeks later.

Eventually, *Chicken Soup for the Soul* hit the number one spot and stayed there for more than a year . . . and in the eyes of the world, this often-rejected manuscript became an "instant bestseller."

Schoolteachers, in particular, loved assigning the book to their students to read, as the stories were easy to absorb and could inspire even the most troubled of students to excel in school and adhere to their goals, no matter how difficult achieving them might seem. It was also a hit with nearly all religious groups, as the stories were inspirational and communicated the strong positive values found at the core of most world religions.

In addition, *Chicken Soup for the Soul* was very popular with sales organizations and large corporations in general. Jack and Mark had somehow captured the essence of what makes America such an inspiring country—stories from everyday people overcoming obstacles in their own lives to reach success, and then reaching out to help others.

It wasn't long before Jack and Mark, along with their publisher, put together *A 2nd Helping of Chicken Soup for the Soul*; and from there they expanded into

Chicken Soup for the Woman's Soul, Chicken Soup for the Teenage Soul, and *Chicken Soup for the Golfer's Soul,* among others. There would eventually come to be more than 200 *Chicken Soup* titles and over 500 million books sold in 47 languages around the world.

Jack loved thinking up new titles and overseeing the development of more and more books with a great team of co-authors and contributors. He knew that he was reaching the tens of millions of people he had always dreamed of reaching, and was now closer to fulfilling his life purpose and destiny.

However, despite the constant media attention and living a life of unexpected superabundance, Jack was deeply conscious of the still-larger purpose for which he had incarnated on planet Earth. He now had the resources, celebrity, and platform to start searching for the other members of the Golden Motorcycle Gang; and to fulfill his dream of helping to heal planet Earth.

TENDER
LOVING CARE

*"Individually, we are one drop.
Together, we are an ocean."*

— RYUNOSUKE SATORO

Thanks to the success of the *Chicken Soup* books, lots of people started appearing in Jack's life. For example, there was Marci Shimoff, who had studied to become a stress-management consultant. After reading *Chicken Soup for the Soul,* Marci and her friend and colleague Jennifer Read Hawthorne came to Jack with the suggestion that they co-author *Chicken Soup for the Woman's Soul* with him. The book was such a success that it led to *Chicken Soup for the Mother's Soul* and several other titles for women, which ultimately sold more than 13 million copies.

Lisa Nichols, who would later go on to great fame as one of the primary teachers in the film *The Secret,* was also introduced to Jack through the *Chicken Soup* book series. Lisa contributed two titles herself: *Chicken Soup for the African American Soul* and *Chicken Soup for the African American Woman's Soul.*

Even Jack's sister, Kimberly Kirberger, approached him with an idea—why not a *Chicken Soup* book for teenagers, in which all the stories were written by teens themselves. *Yes, why not?* thought Jack, and he and Mark published *Chicken Soup for the Teenage Soul,* which sold over six million copies and spawned a dozen more *Teenage Soul* books.

Many others met Jack in a similar manner. The *Chicken Soup* books had become not just a vehicle for Jack to reach millions of people, but also a connector for those who had incarnated, like Jack, as part of the original Golden Motorcycle Gang.

Yet even in the midst of—or perhaps because of—Jack's megasuccess, he still had to deal with the problems that often arise in personal relationships. To that end, Jack's relationship with his second wife, Georgia, began to unravel. They had been living in their dream home in Santa Barbara, California, since 1995;

and had enjoyed a warm and loving relationship for more than 20 years that included the birth of their son, Christopher. They'd had many moments of joy and happiness. However, Jack's devotion to his work, along with his keen focus on his sense of destiny, did not make for the easiest of relationships.

Jack and Georgia eventually saw that their paths were diverging, and they divorced in December 1999. Jack now stepped up the focus on his mission to re-unite the Golden Motorcycle Gang.

It was during a meeting with Marcia Martin (one of the pioneers of the human potential movement) that Jack came up with the idea of creating a special organization that would enable him to share his larger vision of helping humanity.

Jack and Marcia realized that their network of friends and colleagues included some of the most extraordinary human beings on planet Earth, such as Jane Willhite, co-founder of PSI World; Marie Diamond, an international feng shui consultant who specialized in what she called transformational leader-ship training; Marshall Thurber, Bobbi DePorter, and DC Cordova, the co-creators of the "Money & You" program and the Excellerated Business School for Entrepreneurs; and Dr. John Demartini, a self-educated human-behavior specialist who created the Demartini Method and Institute to share the latest breakthroughs in human development with millions. Other members of the network included Michael Bernard Beckwith, John Gray, Lynne Twist, Gay Hendricks, Howard Martin, Paul R. Scheele, Marianne Williamson—and, of course, Jack's longtime friend and mentor, Stewart Emery.

Jack believed that these individuals, and many others, could combine their efforts to make a real and lasting difference in the world. Jack sensed that several of his friends and colleagues might have even been in the original Golden Motorcycle Gang. He wanted to be able to reach out and connect on a regular basis with these likely Golden Motorcycle riders and others who seemed to share his vision. And thus, the Transformational Leadership Council was created.

Known as "TLC" for short, the association with "tender loving care" was intentional. And, of course, the TLC logo was a golden Harley Davidson–like emblem, which would always remind Jack of the Golden Motorcycle Gang.

Originally, membership was limited to people who owned or led transformational training companies;

but eventually it expanded to include the owners of transformational coaching companies, producers of transformational media, and transformational thought leaders. Jack stressed the *transformational* aspect because he understood that only experiential training could create the lasting impact necessary for true change.

Jack had participated in some of the early experiential training courses given in the United States, and he'd personally developed many workshops that taught the process. He'd discovered that this type of training provides actual experiences that have dramatic and lasting impact on each individual's perception of who he or she is and on the true nature of reality—unlike traditional training, which focuses on delivering only concepts and information. Jack knew that people can only be transformed if they have genuine "Aha!" moments that touch not just their intellectual understanding, but their sensory and emotional understanding as well.

Whether through guided visualizations, meditation, or interactive activities with others, Jack felt that experiential training was the only way to achieve lasting breakthroughs in consciousness. He had gone through these experiences himself and had become a master at facilitating them in others. Now, his goal in creating the Transformational Leadership Council was to create a community of teachers and coaches dedicated to creating these experience-based breakthroughs for many more people. Jack recognized that establishing TLC—and creating and developing these communities—was the quickest and most effective path to teach *and* manifest true transformation in others.

Despite Jack's great success, he was somewhat cautious when he sent out invitations to 30 top transformational leaders to meet with him at his home in Santa Barbara. Deep down, he still felt that he wasn't as successful as these people, many of whom had been his mentors and teachers.

Jack's invitation had introduced the concept of forming an association specifically for people who owned their own transformational training companies, as he did. There were associations for all types of specific psychological disciplines, ranging from Gestalt and NLP (neurolinguistic programming) to transactional analysis and EFT (emotional freedom technique)—but as far as Jack could determine, there was no association for those who identified themselves as the owners of transformational training companies.

He had a slight moment of panic after sending out the invitations when he thought that perhaps no one would respond. He was very relieved and overjoyed when all but two of those he had invited confirmed they would be delighted to meet with Jack to explore his concept of creating an organization dedicated to working with other transformational leaders.

At the inaugural meeting, three criteria were established to be a member of TLC:

1. You had to own your own transformational training company. You could not just be a speaker, but had to provide experiential training as part of your work.

2. You had to have your ego in check. There would be no hierarchy, and no one would be accepted if he or she was on an ego trip, and . . .

3. You had to have achieved a high level of financial independence. Jack wanted TLC meetings to be fun and to be held at comfortable resorts at locations throughout the world. He didn't want members who wouldn't be able to join the fun because of the cost.

And TLC *was* equal parts service and fun.

The first meeting was held at John Gray's ranch in Northern California. John had joked that if everyone agreed to hold the first TLC meeting at his ranch, he'd hurry up and make sure that the contractors would finish building out the spa and other amenities. Unfortunately, that didn't happen, and the council's first meeting/party was held with the spa and other amenities far from usable. It didn't matter. The setting was incredibly beautiful, and the members were inspired.

Almost all of the Transformational Leadership Council's members shared Jack's passion and semi-mystical belief that they had a higher purpose to help others transform not just themselves but the planet as well. He realized that somehow he had stumbled on a way to reunite many of the members of the original Golden Motorcycle Gang.

Sparks of positive energy would fly at TLC meetings, with great ideas coming to the forefront as each participant shared his or her unique work and wisdom with the others, and everyone explored how to take their work to the next level and reach even larger audiences. But for Jack, the real significance of TLC was the opportunity to once again be in the presence of the energy of his friends from so long ago.

Jack and his program committee didn't ignore the serious work of creating a powerful agenda for each meeting, or of focusing on the contributions TLC could make to the world—but he couldn't help but simply revel in the camaraderie he shared with his friends from the Golden Motorcycle Gang. The more time he spent with them, the more energy he had, and the more joy he experienced.

Jack saw that in many ways he was still on his solstice break from the Academy of Enlightenment, just having a good time with his friends. Somehow the little diversion of saving this small blue planet in distress had become the quintessence of the joy, challenge, and sense of fun and adventure he and his classmates had been seeking when still in their luminescent form. Taking on human bodies had actually been a thrill. The pleasures of food, drink, sports, lovemaking, and other physical experiences had been unexpected positive consequences of the impulsive decision to perform a good deed that had started the journey.

Jack found that the more he took pleasure in all aspects of being human, the more empathetic and effective he became in his mission as one of the leaders of the Golden Motorcycle Gang. Human beings were now his people and planet Earth was now "his" planet.

SYNCHRONICITY

*"The characteristic feature of all these phenomena,
including . . . synchronistic occurrences, is
meaningful coincidence, and as such I have defined
the synchronistic principle. This principle suggests
that there is an inter-connection or unity of causally
unrelated events, and thus postulates a unitary
aspect of being which can very well be described
as the 'unus mundus' [one world]."*

— DR. CARL JUNG

In the first decade of the 21st century, Jack was enjoying his daily life more than ever, and strongly believed that the Transformational Leadership Council
was making a major contribution to the world. He had
gotten married again—this time to a beautiful woman

named Inga, who shared his new unbridled passion for experiencing life on Earth to its fullest.

However, every day Jack would read the newspaper or watch the news on TV and see that throughout the world, people were in agony. In Africa there were numerous wars and acts of genocide, which, in their savagery and resultant mass suffering, were unrivaled on Earth since perhaps World War II.

In Afghanistan there was constant fighting, with forces inside and outside the country struggling for control for both political and religious purposes. In Asia, the North Koreans were widely seen as a threat to peace—and in response to the treatment given to them by many nations, they were threatening to use nuclear weapons.

The Middle East seemed perpetually in turmoil, eruptions of violence were commonplace, and common ground was nearly impossible to find.

Acts of terror even occurred in the United States, and reminders of the threat of terrorism lurked just about everywhere. Jack's frequent airplane trips, so enjoyable for him in earlier times, were an entirely different experience now. His bags were x-rayed, and his body was frisked to the point that it was as if he might somehow be a terrorist threat himself.

This world seemed rife with division, and not much more at peace with itself than when Jack and his celestial Gang had peered down from the greater skies onto planet Earth in the year 1943.

"Have the Golden Motorcycle Gang and I really made a difference?" Jack asked Inga while out on a walk in their beautiful Santa Barbara garden. Not waiting for a response, he continued, "Is it really possible to save this planet from self-destruction, or has it all just been an illusion that a small group of us can actually make a difference?"

Inga was about to respond when they heard the telephone in the house ring. Jack rushed inside to pick it up, and he heard the voice of his good friend Barbara Marx Hubbard.

"Jack, do you have time to get together this afternoon? Something major is brewing, and I think you are meant to be involved," Barbara said with a sense of excitement and expectation.

Barbara was one of those people whose goodness simply radiated in all she did. Although she had recently turned 81 years of age, the woman was as vibrant and active as she had ever been. She once explained to Jack that in recent months she had somehow received an infusion of energy resulting from the plans now forming in many groups—plans for a major celebration of the "birthing" of a more co-creative, universal humanity on December 21 and 22, 2012.

"Barbara, let me see if I can clear my schedule. I have some videotaping this afternoon, but I think we can meet around 5 P.M. If you wouldn't mind, I think it would be convenient if we meet down by the beach near the Boathouse restaurant, which is where I'll be finishing my last interview," Jack replied.

"Great. That works for me. I'll see you at 5 P.M., unless I hear otherwise from you," Barbara confirmed. Jack smiled, looking forward to meeting his dear friend later.

Jack had been one of the major stars of the hit 2006 film *The Secret*. The movie was reaching tens of millions of people all around the world, and for many it was opening them up to the idea that their own thoughts could make a difference. Jack and his friends had coordinated much of the original filming with other members of the Transformational Leadership Council at a TLC meeting in Aspen, Colorado, in 2005.

With the success of *The Secret,* there were now many filmmakers calling Jack with requests for him to participate in their projects. Many of them had a clearly transformational message, and Jack wanted to help as many as he could, but he also felt he had to be selective. He just had too many commitments . . . so, more often than not, he had to regretfully refuse the numerous requests.

That afternoon, however, he had agreed to be in a film being produced by Gayle Newhouse and Richard Greninger, called *Tapping the Source*. One of the co-producers was Bill Gladstone, an agent, author, and film producer Jack had known for many years.

In fact, Bill was one of the first people to whom he'd revealed his story of the Golden Motorcycle Gang. Jack wasn't sure why he had done so, as Bill was not at that time active in the human potential movement, nor focused on much more than his thriving literary agency. And yet Jack had sensed something innocent and fun about Bill—and when Bill told of his experience of encountering pure bliss in a near-death experience he'd had as a teenager, Jack felt a sense of camaraderie, which inspired him to share his own experience with the Golden Motorcycle Gang before he'd been born on Earth. Since then the two had shared an easy bond, even though they rarely met or worked together.

"Well, that's a wrap. Great interview, Jack, you just nailed the answers," Bill declared with his usual upbeat energy. "Thanks so much for granting the interview. It really means a lot."

"It was my pleasure," Jack assured him. "I really enjoyed it."

"Tell me," Bill said, pulling Jack aside, "has anything happened with the Golden Motorcycle Gang story? I don't think I ever told you this, but that story has stayed with me in an almost mystical way."

"I never knew that story meant so much to you, Bill. A few years back I found a number of small desk clocks in the form of miniature golden motorcycles. I started giving them out to those I thought might have been members of that original Golden Motorcycle Gang. I now only have one of these clocks left, but after this interview and seeing what you are doing with your film, I feel drawn to give it to you. You are obviously part of this work."

"I'm touched and honored. I can't think of any gang I'd rather be a part of," Bill replied, beaming. "In fact, when you first told me about your experience, I began to think I may actually have been part of the original Gang. I am cautious by nature, and probably waited a few extra years, in human terms, to incarnate —but the more time I spend working on projects like *Tapping the Source,* the more I feel that my major mission in life is aligned with yours.

"In the last few years," Bill continued, "I have been focusing more and more on spiritual books, working with clients such as Neale Donald Walsch, Andrew Cohen, Jean Houston, and of course Eckhart Tolle. I have also worked with Dr. Ervin Laszlo, Riane Eisler, L. Hunter Lovins, Dennis Weaver, Thom Hartmann, and other visionaries in the environmental movement. One of my clients for the last decade has been Barbara Marx Hubbard. We just finished interviewing Barbara this morning to capture her thoughts about the meaning of 2012 as a possible window for 'universal humans' to emerge."

"That's really wild," Jack replied, "because I'm meeting Barbara right here in just a few minutes, and she's going to fill me in on her concept of universal humanity and what's to happen in 2012. Why don't you stay and join us? I'm sure she won't mind."

Chapter 13

2012

"It is worthwhile dying, to find out what life is."

— T.S. Eliot

Barbara noticed that the waves were more rhythmic and consistent than usual as she walked up to the table at the Boathouse where Bill and Jack were sitting. Barbara always enjoyed meeting at this particular restaurant because she could be sure to get in a walk along the beach. She found the sound and sight of the waves comforting, and indicative of her connection with all of life and the secrets held by the sea.

Barbara greeted Jack and Bill and flashed her infectious smile.

"I hope it's okay that I invited Bill to join us. He was telling me how he's already plugged into your concept of 2012 as an important transformational date," Jack explained.

"Of course. Bill and I have been working together for more than ten years, and I could tell from the questions he asked me in our interview this morning that he definitely has a role to play as well," Barbara assured Jack, with a soft and generous twinkle in her eyes.

After they ordered some appetizers and a bottle of wine, Barbara got down to the purpose of the meeting. "Jack, we've been friends for many years," she said. "You've helped support my Foundation for Conscious Evolution, and you hosted my 80th birthday party at your home. You share many of my ideas, and your work has always been about helping others. And now, I believe it's time for our greatest adventure yet."

"And what would that be?" Jack asked.

"You just mentioned it: two thousand twelve," Barbara answered.

"Two thousand twelve?" he asked again

"Yes. Two thousand twelve," she reiterated.

"After our interview, Bill explained to me some of the Mayan beliefs about 2012 that he wrote about in his novel *The Twelve*. Is that what you're referring to?" Jack asked, seeking clarification.

"Yes, and no," Barbara responded enigmatically. "Bill captured the essence of the Mayan beliefs about

2012 in his novel. Yet when he wrote his book, he was not aware of the details emerging now with respect to how this window of opportunity that the Mayans predicted can be used in a very practical way to ensure that the positive aspects of the Mayan prophecy will indeed come true.

"Many people who are being quoted in the media are predicting cataclysmic doom and destruction," she continued. "But I believe 2012 can be the beginning of a positive evolutionary day—and to support that happening, I think we need to dramatize what is currently working toward the creation of planetary culture, a co-creative society. From an evolutionary point of view, it is clear that what we need at this time is a convergence of what is creative, loving, and innovative in the world; and this would be a perfect time to create it."

"Barbara was explaining this to me earlier this morning," Bill reported. "As I told her, when I was an anthropologist at Harvard, I studied many different cultures from all over the globe, and I learned that it wasn't just the Mayans who believed that 2012 is a pivotal year. In many of these cultures—including the Tibetan, Hawaiian, Hopi, and Hindu; as well as many indigenous traditions from time immemorial—there has been a prediction that at just about this time, a new golden age will occur for all humanity. This age has different names in each culture, but most of them share the belief that somehow humans will become more spiritual beings, and facilitating this transformation is the center of Barbara's most recent work. She sees that we are evolving from our self-centered adolescent state to our spirit-centered, co-creative, universal stage as a natural evolutionary path."

"That is exactly right," Barbara confirmed.

"I've heard many people talk about 2012," Jack joined in, "but you two are the first to explain it in a way that actually resonates with me. I have never believed that the world will end in 2012, and I certainly don't believe in the end-time scenarios of an impending apocalypse—but from everything I've been reading and learning, I *do* share a sense of urgency about the state of the world and the need for immediate action. And when we first met, Bill told me he had a vision similar to my Golden Motorcycle Gang experience when he related his near-death experience to me."

"My vision was not exactly similar," Bill explained. "However, my near-death experience gave me a sense of purpose that was heightened when I heard Jack talk about the Golden Motorcycle Gang. I do think the two experiences are linked, and that these experiences somehow connect with what you've been promoting as Conscious Evolution ever since I have known you, Barbara."

Smiling while drinking her wine, Barbara responded, "Bill, please tell me about your near-death experience. I also had a life-altering experience as a young woman, which totally connected me with my life purpose. I'm finding that near-death and other unusual experiences can be great guides for people uncovering their roles in the larger pattern of the whole."

"When I was 15 years old, I was in a doctor's office and was given some medication and then told to sit down while the doctor went to check on another patient," Bill began. "I remember my conscious awareness floated up to the top of the ceiling of the room. Then 'I' was greeted by 12 entities who surrounded me in an aura of love. I experienced a level of bliss and security that was beyond description. Then I saw 12 colors and the tunnel of white light that so many people who have had near-death experiences have described in their accounts.

"Suddenly, I heard a loud noise and noticed a man kneeling on the floor, who was the source of the noise. I next noticed that the man was wearing a white coat, as doctors did in those days, and I reflected that the man was a doctor. Then I realized that the doctor was trying to get the attention of an inert body lying on the floor. My first thought was, *Why won't that body respond to the doctor so he won't be so upset?* My next thought was, *Oh, that's my body. I better get back into it so that doctor will feel better.*"

"Fascinating," was Barbara's observation. "What happened next?"

"Well, I was suddenly in my body again, and I looked up and saw the doctor's facial expression go from panic to relief. 'I thought we'd lost you,' he told me, with alarm in his eyes. 'You turned green and had no pulse. You must have had a reaction to the penicillin.' Once he realized I wasn't going to die, he relaxed. He had me stay there for a while for observation, and then let me go home."

"What conclusions did you draw from your experience?"

"I was only 15 at the time, and at first I was full of enthusiasm, thinking that I'd been given important information that I needed to share with others. But when I started sharing my experience of the 'white light' and my new personal knowledge of the true eternal nature of consciousness, I was confronted with skepticism and negative responses. Many people immediately wanted to provide a scientific explanation of how the oxygen to my brain had been cut off and that I had hallucinated the entire experience.

"Others assured me that only God or a divine being could have had this level of communication with 'beings from the other side,' so I soon learned it was best not to discuss my near-death experience with others," Bill continued. "This was long before the publication of Dr. Raymond Moody's book *Life After Life*, so for most people, even talking about these kinds of experiences was the equivalent of saying that you'd gone through an alien abduction. I was an A-plus student, captain of my football and baseball teams, and I wanted to maintain my status as a 'regular guy' and not be considered a kook."

"Interesting that you mention *Life After Life*," Jack chimed in. "I read it when I was in graduate school, and it was a life-changing book for me. I was so intrigued by Moody and his work that I wrote a major report on the phenomenon of near-death experiences. It opened me up to accepting the reality of altered states of awareness as relatively common. That book also allowed me to draw out stories from people who, without the context of knowing that these unusual states of consciousness occur to others, would ignore or refuse to talk about their own experiences. In many instances these repressed stories and incidents represented critical life-changing moments for them.

"Just like you, Bill, many people have reported these amazing encounters—or transcendent experiences, as I prefer to call them—and then not allowed them to influence their lives. It's almost as if they're being given huge wake-up calls and then disregard the alarm clock and just go back to sleep. For me, Moody's book changed the way I thought about teaching. I realized that the ultimate 'final exam' at the end of life is about how much you have learned about love and helping others."

"Jack, that is exactly why we need to celebrate the New Birth!" Barbara exclaimed enthusiastically. "People are waking up, but they need support. They need to realize that their own critical breakthroughs in consciousness and creativity are not deviant or weird, but rather part of a new norm. But I'd like to hear the rest of your story, Bill, and why it has piqued your interest in 2012."

"At first my near-death experience didn't have any connection at all with 2012," Bill admitted. "I actually spent many years ignoring the experience altogether. When I first sat down to write my novel, I was thinking about the apocalyptic 'end-time' as described in the Bible as the climax for my story. I did see a connection between the 12 apostles and the 12 energies that came to me in my near-death experience, but there was no thought of 2012 at all.

"In fact, I started writing the novel in 1979, and that was before José Argüelles had created the million-person Harmonic Convergence event—which, in the late 1980s, began to draw attention to the importance of December 21, 2012, as the end of the Mayan calendar. Because I was raising a family and running a relatively large literary agency, I really had no time to work on finishing my novel until late 2008. By then the connection with the second coming of Christ in the year 2000, which was the end point in my original draft, was way out of date, so I made a decision to switch the climax to 2012. That's when I started doing research on why so many people had become fascinated with that date."

"It's true, whether it's a new Hollywood movie or a History Channel special, 2012 seems to be one of the hot topics of the day. I've even noticed entire shelves of books about 2012 at the local Barnes & Noble," Jack confirmed.

Nodding, Bill continued. "I read everything I could about 2012, including books debunking the phenomenon as a complete myth. I also read books supporting the traditional Mayan message from scholars such as John Major Jenkins, Gregg Braden, and Daniel

Pinchbeck; but it wasn't until I had finished the first draft of my novel that I learned of my own special relationship to December 21, 2012. In my novel, I wanted to be sure that the 12 protagonists represented every major world religion and ethnic background in the world. I decided that I'd go one step further and check out the numerological values of the names of the characters, since I wanted to be sure that each name represented one of the nine primary numbers. The numerologist who did this work for me gave me the startling news that I would not have to change a single name to cover all of the nine energies. That was probably only a one-in-one-thousand chance 'occurrence.'"

"How can names have numerological values?" Jack asked.

"I'm not an expert myself, but the numerologist explained how every letter in the alphabet has a number value, and that all she needed to do was to add up the number values from each letter in each name in the novel. The name 'Al' would be a 4, since the number value of A is 1 and the number value of L is 12. You add 1 and 12 and get 13, and then add 1 and 3 and you get 4. There are only 9 basic numbers, so you have to keep adding until you only have a number value of 9 or less," Bill explained.

"I'm not a mathematician, but I can see why having 12 random names reduce to the 9 basic numbers
got your attention," Jack commented.

"It sure did, but what really shocked me was when
the numerologist explained that she had also com-
pared the numbers for the birthday of Max Doff, the
protagonist of the novel—December 12, 1949—with
the numbers contained in the end date of the Mayan
calendar—December 21, 2012. I hadn't really thought
about asking about that connection, even though the
novel was written to end on that precise date. What
she told me blew me away."

After a brief pause, Bill went on. "The numerologist went through the calculations and explained that
the numbers were a perfect match. The odds against a
perfect match for a birthday with 12/12—which was
necessary given the plot of the novel with the exact
number value of 12/21/2012—were, she estimated,
almost one in a million. The combination of the
two events, the names representing the nine basic
numbers, and the birthday of the protagonist being
identical to the number value of December 21, 2012,
represented a mathematical chance occurrence of one
in a billion. What she didn't know, which amazed me

even more, is that I had chosen my actual birthday—which is December 12, 1949—as the birthday for Max Doff."

Jack hummed a few bars from *The Twilight Zone* theme song, indicating his awareness of the eerie nature of these coincidences. And then Barbara exclaimed, "What an amazing synchronicity! I never knew this about your birthday, but you must realize that my birthday—December 22—represents the first day of the new 26,000-year cycle that starts on December 22, 2012. Our birthdays are linked, Bill. I am now more certain than ever that you are also meant to be part of our team."

A PLANETARY SMILE

"Peace starts with a smile."

— MOTHER TERESA

"It is remarkable how a seemingly small detail such as a date or a street address or a phone number can be such a clear marker," Jack observed. "I can now see Bill's connection and his enthusiasm for focusing on 2012 as a pivotal date. But, Barbara, you said earlier that you would tell us about the experience you had as a girl that got you started on your initial journey."

"I really have had two remarkable—what some might consider 'out of body'—experiences that have been critical in my awareness of my life purpose," Barbara responded.

"Even as a very young girl I wanted to understand how we could use the tremendous power of our nuclear technology for good. Although I was only a teenager when atomic bombs were used against the Japanese, it made me stop and think.

"In 1952, when I was still in college, I had the opportunity to meet with President Dwight Eisenhower, who was a friend of my father. I asked the President, 'What is the potential of our new power and technology that is good?' To my dismay, he had no answer. He just replied, 'I do not know. I have no idea.'

"In that moment I thought to myself that if the President of the United States, the most powerful man in the world, had no idea, then somebody better find out. And for many years I was one of the people trying to do so.

"I co-founded the Committee for the Future in Washington, D.C., and I was also instrumental in founding the World Future Society. In my advocacy for a positive future, I met Buckminster Fuller, Abraham Maslow, and many other powerful leaders.

"One day, Dr. Jonas Salk called me up out of the blue and invited me to lunch! Jonas had read an article I had written and was moved to meet with me. He explained that he felt I was among several visionaries of the post–World War II generation who were filled with a mysterious sense of the future and a desire to give their best for the good of all. Jonas was emphatic that people like me were needed for humankind to evolve to its next level. This recognition from Jonas started me on my path as an evolutionary woman, learning that we are all part of the greater process of creation."

After taking a sip of her wine, Barbara went on. "One afternoon in 1966, in the midst of searching, reading, and meeting with key people, I took my usual walk. Suddenly, a great question arose in my mind.

"I had been reading Reinhold Niebuhr on the theme of community, and he had been quoting the biblical statement in Corinthians that all of us are members of one body. With that quote in mind, and filled with so many ideas that were not fully assimilated, I stopped and raised my face upward to the universe and demanded 'I want to know our story. What on Earth is comparable to the story of the birth of Christ? What story, if we knew it, would make the difference for our generation the way the Gospels have for 2,000 years?'

"My mind's eye—what Bill called in his near-death experience 'my conscious awareness'—immediately went into outer space, as if I were an astronaut looking down on planet Earth. I saw the Earth struggling to coordinate. I felt the Earth running out of energy and resources. I felt the shared pain that existed through-out the entire planet, in both animals and humans as well as in plants and even the rocks and soil. I felt myself as one with all of life, and I felt the unity of all life, and of Earth as a single body of which we are all but a part.

"Suddenly, as if in a movie, the scene of present-day Earth suffering shifted to a future time. I realized that the pain was a signal that woke us up! I felt empathy pouring forth throughout the entire planet. I felt people helping each other, *healing* each other. I saw breakthroughs in health, education, energy, business, environment, and media. I saw collaboration among all peoples and all fields. I saw the reality that when human beings connected with their genius and their ability to innovate, the Earth had sufficient resources to feed, house, educate, and sustain all life on her. I felt that when our innovations all connect, we really are one planetary body.

"In that moment, it was as though all humanity breathed one coordinated breath together."

Barbara continued, "In that moment I felt mystic light arising from all people on Earth, and with that shared breath, a wonderful tone was heard—a vibration that linked us all in resonance, in a moment of global heart-coherence. This breath and tone generated a vibration of joy that resonated in the hearts of tens of millions of human beings. Collectively, we experienced lights from the universe coming toward us . . . almost ready for 'contact.' But we were still too young as a species. It was as if we had just, as a planetary collective, opened our eyes for the first time and experienced our first 'planetary smile.'

"Then I heard these words: 'Our story is the birth of a universal humanity. What all the great avatars came to Earth to reveal is true. We are one body. We are being born. We are whole, we are good, and we are universal. Go tell the story of the birth of a universal humanity, Barbara!'"

Jack smiled and said, "That is a powerful story. Your words remind me of my own sense that we are truly all one. I have experienced this many times in my own meditations and as I travel around the world—that we are all like cells in a larger body of one humanity."

Barbara continued, "This spiritual experience changed my life forever. At first I wasn't certain how to go about telling the story of the birth of a universal humanity. I studied cosmology, history, science, and art. I became a speaker and a writer. Then Buckminster Fuller asked me to take these ideas of a positive future into the political arena.

"So, in 1983, I launched a campaign to be nominated for Vice President on the Democratic ticket. The campaign was so successful that at the 1984 Democratic National Convention, which was held in San Francisco, I actually became the other woman whose name was placed in nomination along with Geraldine Ferraro. Of course, *she* was ultimately selected as Walter Mondale's running mate, but I was given an opportunity to address the delegates and formally present my vision for a social function to be developed in the office of the Vice President. It was to be a 'Peace Room,' which would focus on, scan for, map, connect, and communicate what is *working* in America and the world. It was a description of what I had seen in my vision as the first step for the birth of a universal humanity."

"What amazes me is that you had this insight so many years ago," Bill noted. "It is only in the last several years that I've even encountered other visionaries talking about what is referred to as 'Conscious Evolution.' Your story of the birth of a universal humanity is close to what spiritual teacher Andrew Cohen calls being an 'evolutionary.' In his magazine *Enlighten-Next,* he publishes articles that talk about some of the kinds of things you were trying to do decades before, Barbara.

"Andrew sees an opportunity for each human being to spiritually awaken to the energy and intelligence behind the evolutionary process," Bill continued, "and to take action to enhance the evolutionary pattern that is already in process. In his words, if you care about the future of humanity and our planet, then it is up to you to forge that future through your own spiritual evolution and your conscious, creative relationships with others. That's what it means to be an evolutionary."

"Andrew and I have discussed these ideas at length during sessions of the Evolutionary Leaders conferences with Deepak Chopra and Marianne Williamson and others," Barbara confirmed. "The goal of Evolutionary Leaders is to share these ideas with as many people as possible. We all feel a sense of urgency that each of us is part of the evolving pattern, and that we each have a responsibility to share this message at this exact moment in human history. I personally feel that telling the story of what is being born on planet Earth at this time by and through us is vital to the manifestation of the birth itself.

"On the simplest level, people can only see and hear what they have been prepared to see and hear. For example, it has been reported that the original Peruvian and Mexican peoples were unable to observe the tall ships of the first Europeans who conquered them. They had no concept that such ships could exist. Until the average person can understand the story of the birth of a new planetary culture, which allows each of us to experience our individual sense of connection with each other and the divine, the actual manifestation of this planetary culture is impossible."

"I don't want to trivialize what you're saying, but it sounds a little like a quote from former New York Yankee Yogi Berra, who was famous for his malapropisms, one being 'I wouldn't have seen it if I hadn't believed it,'" Bill joked.

"No, that's okay," Barbara responded. "That saying has more truth to it than Mr. Berra could have realized. We can't expect people to change their behavior and take action toward a new goal until they understand the story behind the goal. That is why this telling of the story is so important, and that is why I am counting on both of you and others to help spread the word."

"Of course we want to help, Barbara," Jack replied, "but I must ask: Why now? What has happened recently that has given you this renewed sense of urgency and enthusiasm?"

"To answer that question, I need to explain my other mystical experience that occurred more recently, when I was in Maui in March of 2003. I know the exact date because I keep a journal in which I record my most profound thoughts and experiences. I read from my diaries once a year or so, and I just recently reread this particular entry," Barbara explained, and then turned and addressed Jack directly. "You and I are even more connected than we had realized. After you hear this story, I think you'll know why the Golden Motorcycle Gang has been such a lasting vision for you and has now become such an important concept in your life."

Jack was immediately intrigued. He poured another glass of wine for everyone at the table, and settled back to listen to Barbara's story.

THE FIVE QUESTIONS

*"A small body of determined spirits
fired by an unquenchable faith in their
mission can alter the course of history."*

— MAHATMA GANDHI

Barbara looked out at the ocean she loved so much, enjoyed some more wine, and resumed her story.

"In February of 2003 I'd had an appendicitis attack," she told Jack and Bill. "I went to the hospital, and the operation to remove my appendix was completely successful. However, in analyzing my blood cells after the operation, the doctors discovered that I had an abnormally high count of white blood cells.

White blood cells are good, but too many of them can ultimately shut down the body. My condition was considered a form of chronic leukemia, not something that would pose an immediate danger to my life, but a condition that I needed to address. I was encouraged to take action to lower my white-blood-cell count.

"I decided to go on vacation to Maui, one of my favorite places in the entire world, to work with a healer who lives there. I wanted to see if there might be an emotional link to my overproduction of white blood cells. The healer advised me to let her take me on a full-life regression that would release any emotional blocks that might be the root cause of what was happening with me physically.

"I was 73 years old at the time, so we started with that year—I was asked to look over the past year and see if there was anyone or any incident that I needed to forgive. Then I was asked to look at my 72nd year, and then my 71st . . . and all the way back through my young adulthood, my teenage years, my early childhood, and right up to my birth.

"For each year, I was able to remember a person or an experience that might benefit from my forgiveness; and as I remembered and forgave each person and each experience, I started to feel lighter and lighter and more and more joyous. I had so much to be grateful for, so many wonderful people who had tried to help me along the path of my life—but, of course, many of them had at times behaved in ways that had, at least in the moment, hurt me or caused me pain.

"And I also recognized moments in my life when I had—perhaps through overzealousness in my pursuit of my own goals—been hurtful to others. It felt wonderful to forgive others and myself, and I was experiencing greater and greater euphoria with each year that I relived, remembered, and forgave.

"I went back in my mind to my very own birth, and then to my experience in my mother's womb, and then to my conception, and then even before conception. I saw myself in ancient Greece, in a setting that reminded me of the descriptions I had read of the Elysian Fields.

"In the background, I saw Plato, Aristotle, and then many other ascended masters and avatars. I was with a group, and we were all sitting on a ledge, as though we were getting ready to 'jump off' together. We were volunteering to come to Earth for the birth of a universal humanity. Each of us had a part of the whole plan. We were to find each other and reassemble at the precise moment when the planetary birth process was actually happening. We would feel a sense of affinity upon finding each other. Once on Earth, our mission would be to reconnect with the other members of our group, and with additional groups to ensure a healthy birth."

Jack could not remain quiet any longer. "Barbara, this is almost identical to what I experienced when I imagined myself cruising through the universe with my friends on our golden motorcycles before my own conception!" he interrupted.

"I know, but I never made the connection until Bill reminded me of this, just after I'd been rereading my diaries earlier this morning. But wait, you need to hear the rest of the story."

Jack drew his chair closer to the table and gave Barbara his full attention.

"When I experienced being in what I call the Greek Elysian Fields with these masters and avatars," she continued, "I looked around at those volunteering with me and tried to see if I could recognize any of them. I couldn't, but I felt an energy that was familiar and comfortable. As the meeting ended, I was given five questions and told that I was to ask these questions to those I met on Earth. In so doing I would assist in not only reassembling the group, but in inspiring those who had entered contracts to remember who they were and what their mission was."

Barbara paused to take a sip of wine.

"The suspense is killing me," Bill blurted out. "What were the five questions?"

Barbara pulled out a beautiful notebook, which had "Barbara Marx Hubbard Journals for 2003–2004" in clear script on the cover.

"I was rereading this journal this morning, which is the reason I called Jack today. I wrote down the questions word for word the very same day I had my full life-regression session. Let me read them to you."

"Yes, please do," Jack urged.

Barbara read from her notebook:

"Question Number One: What do you know of the original plan?

"Question Number Two: Do you have any memory of having volunteered to be of service to Earth at this particular time?

"Question Number Three: If so, do you remember your contract?

"Question Number Four: What do you do best in the world that only you can do?

"Question Number Five: What are you to do now, and what tools or resources do you need to do it?"

Jack didn't say a word. He was overwhelmed by how the questions were so related to his own experience as a member of the Golden Motorcycle Gang.

Breaking the silence, Bill said, "When I first heard Jack's story of the Golden Motorcycle Gang, I immediately felt the sense that he was describing the way the universe really works. Of course, for most people it's just a story, but for me it made me feel that I was not alone, that others had a similar way of seeing the world and their role here. I always felt, even as a very young child, that I had a larger purpose.

"And now to hear your story, Barbara, it makes me feel that this really is the new story that humanity has been waiting for. Maybe there is something we can all do together in 2012 that *will* make a positive difference."

Then Jack spoke. "Barbara, you never cease to inspire me. I have always resonated with you and the work you're doing through your foundation, and your experience in the Elysian Fields is so similar to my own with the Golden Motorcycle Gang. The questions you were told to ask are the key questions we all need to be asking ourselves and each other at this time. Each of us needs to analyze what we do best and what our unique gift is. Even more important, we need to analyze what we are each able to contribute at this precise moment, and we must ask each other for the resources we need to be successful.

"Through the groups I am closely aligned with—the Transformational Leadership Council, the Evolutionary Leaders, the Bioneers, the Pachamama Alliance, Four Years. Go.—and other similar organizations, we can reach many gifted people."

Barbara replied, "And these people will have other organizations with which they are affiliated. Some of the groups we will know, others we won't know, and still others will emerge in the next year. What they'll all share is that the story we're telling is one that will resonate with each of them as profoundly as we are sharing it today."

"And the more groups and people we have in alignment, the greater the momentum we will have, the more resources will be dedicated, and the more certain each of us will become that this moment is ours to achieve. It will be the ultimate demonstration of strength in numbers, and for the right cause; across borders, across oceans, across languages and cultures—which may just be the first such instance in human history."

"Exactly, Jack!" Barbara exclaimed. "We will reassemble the original Golden Motorcycle Gang, as well as all the other groups that have chosen to be born to assist in the birth of what I describe as 'the new story of humanity.' It's not so much about creating a new belief system as becoming aware of a natural patterning process toward what is already emerging. Although the signs of disruption are clear, there is also an emerging sense of greater harmony and creativity, and many groups are already aware of this positive pattern. Our job is to help identify these groups and help them connect with each other."

VIDEO MESSAGE FROM
Barbara Marx Hubbard

SNAP A MOBILE PIC

Ez.com/bhubbard

NEED MOBILE READER?
EZ.com/getreader

BIRTH DAY–
PARTY PLANS

*"Never doubt that a small group of thoughtful,
committed individuals can change the world.
Indeed, it's the only thing that ever has."*

— MARGARET MEAD

The sun was starting to set over the Pacific Ocean,
but neither Jack nor Bill was ready to leave the Boathouse.

"What did you just say, Barbara?" Jack asked, even
though he had clearly heard her.

"I said we need to start planning for the largest
Birth Day party in the history of the world."

"That's what I thought you said," he confirmed.

"You know, Jack and Bill, this is not an entirely new idea. There were more than a million people who celebrated José Argüelles's Harmonic Convergence in the late 1980s; and, of course, there were millions of people worldwide, perhaps hundreds of millions, who celebrated the beginning of the new millennium on December 31, 1999. These individuals saw those dates as not just new years, but as the dawning of something new for humanity. What this 'new thing' might be wasn't clear then for many of them, but the remarkable thing is that this feeling of something extraordinary taking place hasn't gone away . . . it's only deepened and taken root over the last decade. And finally, so many people—in fact, so many people who the three of us know—are ready to shepherd in the new era, to make it a reality."

Barbara went on. "It could be the largest celebration of what is new, emerging, innovative, and working toward 'a world that works for everyone,' as Buckminster Fuller put it. We should connect and highlight all the positive organizations and initiatives that are facilitating the shift in consciousness.

"I think this 'due date' has been offered by history itself. Some of us began to realize that since December 21, 2012, is considered the end of the 26,000-year cycle, then naturally, December 22 is clearly the beginning of the next cycle.

"It's not by accident that Stephen Dinan of the Shift Network asked me to teach a course called 'the Agents of Conscious Evolution Training' to create part of a global team to actually help organize such an event. He is calling the celebration 'Birth 2012: Cocreating a Planetary Shift.' This will be an event of mass coherence and connectivity. Stephen is serving as a 'producer' of sorts of this global media event on December 22, and it is our hope and expectation that many millions of people will participate."

"That is a huge undertaking," Jack remarked.

"Yes, it is. That's why we need your help, Jack. I was told in my meditations when I was given the five questions that I would connect with someone of world stature who would be able to use his influence to gather the many millions we will need to initiate the birth of a new world.

"The present 26,000-year cycle ends on December 21, 2012, and the new cycle begins on December 22, 2012. The new cycle is the first day of our New Earth. I think Eckhart Tolle must have intuitively understood the reality of the actual birthing of a New Earth when he chose it to be the title for his book, which Oprah used for her webcast classes in 2008. Along with

Eckhart, I can sense that a new consciousness is arising in us as individuals and collectively.

"However, it is not just the Birth Day for a new universal humanity but the Birth Day for a New Earth itself, an Earth that is being born into a higher vibration. Even though this process has already started and will continue for many years and decades after December 22, 2012, I think it's essential that we celebrate that specific day," Barbara explained.

"With me, you're preaching to the choir," Bill responded with enthusiasm. "I am absolutely convinced that December 22, 2012, is the beginning of a new vibration. In fact, that's exactly why I wrote my novel. During my research I learned from John Major Jenkins about the wobble and rotation of the Earth, which requires 26,000 years to complete a full rotation. How the Mayans came up with their own 26,000–year time period for their calendar, without any advanced scientific measuring instruments, amazes me."

Jack mused, "That is an inexplicable coincidence, but a lot of people are predicting that December 21, 2012, is going to be a time of cataclysmic physical destruction on Earth: earthquakes, tsunamis, volcanic eruptions—possibly even nuclear war. Do we really want to link such an important event and celebration as the Birth Day to a time when there might be major cataclysms occurring?"

"What you say is true. Those predictions are out there, but that is just the reason to focus on this date," Barbara asserted. "The media is doing us a favor by airing all the reports both promoting the doom and gloom and debunking it. Because of the movies and TV shows and newscasts, the world is already focusing on this specific date. We already have the attention of millions of people, and we can build on this media attention in a positive way.

"As I mentioned, I am involved with the Agents of Conscious Evolution Training with Stephen Dinan and the Shift Network. It's the most popular course we've ever given. More than 20,000 people attended the initial webinar. That is the biggest audience I have addressed since the Democratic National Convention in 1984, which was aired on national television. With your outreach, Jack, I can assure you that once you start letting others know that you see a positive opportunity to use 2012 to raise their awareness, you will have millions of people wanting to participate in the celebration."

"But why do we need a celebration?" Jack asked. "I love the five questions, and I share your sense that we must reassemble the Golden Motorcycle Gang and other groups that have incarnated for the goal of facilitating personal and collective evolution. I'm just wondering if a celebration—which is going to cost millions of dollars to organize and countless hours of effort from tens of thousands of people—is really going to make a difference."

"Celebrations are important," Barbara replied. "Births have been celebrated throughout history in every culture in the world. In this instance we are talking about the birth of a new planetary culture, a new civilization of harmony and cooperation that is already arising in our midst. We need to identify and celebrate the positive innovations and creativity of humanity. Many individuals will doubt that this is real, and one of the best ways to show that it *is* real is to have millions of people recognize the date and participate in their own rituals so that they feel a part of the birth—and even more important, part of the community that will support the newborn planet. Everyone could be asked what his or her gift is to this planetary celebration. It could be a worldwide demonstration of creativity and heart-coherence."

"Okay, I can understand that," Jack said with a nod. "I also understand the principle of coherence, which my friends Doc Childre, Howard Martin, and Deborah Rozman at the Institute of HeartMath have been studying. They have reported that when millions of people focus on common goals, they create resonance patterns that can have a major energetic impact on events in the material world. But I still have to ask, is this really the best date and the best way to create this resonance?"

"We can never know for sure, but we do know that time is running out," Barbara responded. "I hope that December 22, 2012, becomes but the first of decades and millennia of Birth Day celebrations for the New Earth. The peoples of the planet share so much more than we ever acknowledge, yet all too often our celebrations are only in observance of 'national holidays' or affiliated with religions, which are never universal. Why not usher in a 'global holiday,' one that celebrates and amplifies what we share—which is, after all, a common destiny on the same planet?

"We have very little time left to switch the dynamics that have led to the crises on the planet. Many of us realize that the Birth Day is simply the beginning of an ongoing process. We will need a website to collect and share the stories of people's successes, solutions, and breakthroughs. We either cooperate with this new evolution or we will experience the opposite, which is devolution. Devolution will bring on a massive destruction of life on Earth.

"We are already seeing the destructive impact of global warming, with the melting of the ice caps, tornadoes, hurricanes, floods, tsunamis, and earthquakes. We are also seeing economic breakdowns, widespread revolutions throughout the Middle East, and political turmoil throughout Africa. There is the very real possibility of the extinction of our species," Barbara stated with conviction.

Jack's resistance started to melt away. "I see your point. Even if December 22, 2012, is not a real date for the actual birth of a New World and a new consciousness, it is a date around which we can organize flash mobs, concerts, demonstrations, workshops, humanitarian projects, group meditations, peace initiatives, and experiences to raise conscious awareness."

"Exactly. It's not even that mysterious. Something new is being born through all of us. This convergence of belief and inspiration among so many people, apart from anything that will physically happen to the Earth, is itself a phenomenon we cannot ignore and must recognize and celebrate. The old world *is* passing away. That is the beauty of this celebration of December 22, 2012; it can literally become true. It depends on what all of us do. But this much we know: we *are* all one, and as one we can absolutely become aware of ourselves as universal humans on December 22, 2012."

"Barbara, I'm thinking about what you said a few hours ago," Bill offered with enthusiasm. "You said that in 1969 you had a vision where all humanity breathed one coordinated breath together. We're talking about creating the circumstances where exactly that breath can occur."

"That's right, Bill, and we need to remember that from the perspective of a planetary culture, we are still very young—but that we are also adults able to organize a celebration for what is being born through all of us, for our own birth into a New World. Even if we only believe that December 22, 2012, is but a symbolic Birth Day, it is essential that we use this date to create the resonance that might turn our desire into a reality. We have nothing to lose and much to gain," Barbara concluded, feeling she now had Jack's full support.

"Barbara Marx Hubbard, you are an irresistible force of nature!" Jack exclaimed with a huge smile.

"No more than you," Barbara replied with a laugh.

The sun had now set, but the afterglow of pinks and purples was glistening in a perfect sky above the rhythmic waves of the Pacific Ocean, which were pounding gently on the shore next to the Boathouse. Jack looked at the sky and then at Barbara, breathed a

145

sigh of acceptance and joy, and told her, "This is going to be a big job, but I will do all I can to help."

"You have no idea how grateful I am. This is truly a dream come true," she responded, her voice filled with joy.

"No, Barbara, it is I who must be grateful to you. I know that all the members of the Golden Motorcycle Gang incarnated to take on a monumental task, and I think this is going to be a wonderful opportunity for me and the other members to help fulfill our own missions and our destinies; what your friends in the Elysian Fields called 'our contracts.'"

Bill had been listening with rapt attention to the entire conversation. Now he said, "I'm not sure what my role is, but I'm definitely here to help. We have an interview with Jane Willhite scheduled for tomorrow morning, but if you two plan on meeting tomorrow, I would love to stay over and offer my support."

"Oh my gosh. I had totally forgotten about the time," Jack acknowledged. "Jane is actually staying with us at the house tonight, and no doubt Inga is holding dinner and waiting for me. Let's pick this up tomorrow after your filming. I definitely think you should be in the meeting, Bill, so if it's okay with you, I'll tell Jane that you'll shoot the interview at my house so we can save time. And I'll invite her to join us for our conversation as well. She's a founding member of the Transformational Leadership Council, and I'm sure she'll be a good sounding board for our first brainstorming session."

As Jack rose from the table and paid the bill, he gazed again at the sky, now darker but still glowing, and he felt only joy.

A SILVER
MOTORCYCLE
RIDER

*"The crisis, as well as the opportunity, of our time
is to surrender the controlling aspects of our ego
and its conditioned fear mechanisms to the primary
torsion energy of unconditional love that is seeking
to evolve us and is calling us as a species home."*

— SOL LUCKMAN

When Jack returned home, he found his wife,
Inga, and Jane Willhite in the living room having a
glass of chardonnay.

"Come join us, Jack. Jane has been telling me about her newest grandchildren and what's been happening up at Clearlake. You're more than an hour late. I hope everything's all right," Inga chided mischievously.

Jack gave his wife and then Jane a big hug as he sat down and poured himself a glass of wine. "Everything is great. I was just meeting with Barbara Marx Hubbard, and we had a lot to catch up on. She's an amazing woman with some very big plans for the future. She's over 80 now, yet she just keeps going. She's a real inspiration to me on many levels," he replied.

"I love Barbara," Jane said. "She's been a real inspiration to my work with PSI as well."

"Really? How so?" Jack asked.

"When my husband, Thomas, and I created PSI World, I was clear that this not-for-profit foundation had to be for the betterment of humankind—and that we had to focus on the entire world, not just a specific cause or place. I've spent the best part of the last decade thinking about ways to integrate the leadership training we're doing at PSI so that we can train young people to be future leaders, not just for their own success, but for the betterment of the planet as a whole. In fact, that was one of the reasons I wanted to visit with you . . . and, by the way, thanks so much for putting me up for the night."

"Oh, it's our pleasure to have you. You so rarely leave Northern California," Inga commented.

Jane smiled. "Well, as you know, I'm being taped for a film tomorrow. Bob Proctor and Berny Dohrmann called me up and just insisted I be in this film, *Tapping the Source*. I generally like to stay in the background, but they both feel it's time for me to be in front of the camera and share what we're doing at PSI. Normally I would have said no, but I do feel a real sense of urgency if we're going to make a difference on the scale Thomas envisioned for PSI when he was still with us so many years ago."

Jack had a sip of wine and reassured Jane, "I just finished being interviewed for *Tapping the Source* myself this afternoon. The film is focusing on the law of attraction more as the law of love and service than as a principle just to manifest personal material abundance. I'm sure you'll enjoy being interviewed. I did."

"That's good to know, since I was somewhat reluctant at first. I only want to be part of projects that can make a true difference. You know, when I agreed to be a founding member of the Transformational Leadership Council, I wanted to be sure that we would find ways to be of greater service to others and not just create an organization to further our own immediate business goals. I'm pleased with what we've been able

151

to accomplish so far, but that is one of the things I wanted to talk with you about, Jack. How do we take TLC to the next level so that we can ensure that the next generation of leaders can fast-track what our work is revealing about manifesting transformation on a global level?"

"I'm not sure I have an immediate answer—but I think that Barbara's latest idea to utilize December 22, 2012, as a marker for what she is calling 'the new story for humanity' might be one way of connecting with future leaders on a massive scale. Barbara's working with a rapidly growing group through Stephen Dinan's Shift Network. She told me that they hope to have ten million or more people participate, and Barbara and Stephen are counting on TLC to help generate participants," Jack responded.

"Leave it to Barbara. That woman always thinks big," Inga noted with a laugh.

"Ten million people," Jane whistled. "Wow! But if anyone can do it, it will be Barbara. Tell me more."

"I would like to hear the details as well, but let's move on to dinner," Inga urged. "Everything's been ready for the last hour, and I'm sure we're all famished."

The three of them moved toward the dining room and enjoyed an exquisite dinner. As they ate, Jack

brought his wife and friend up to date on the idea of a celebration for all humanity to help usher in the next phase of evolution as universal humans.

Inga brought out a wonderful fruit-salad dessert with kiwi, pineapple, blueberries, and other delicacies. "Let me get this straight," she said. "Is the point of the celebration just that everyone on planet Earth on December 22 celebrates having survived the Mayan calendar—and in so doing, automatically become more enlightened beings? Or is there something more to it?"

"Barbara seemed very clear that there's more to it," Jack confirmed. "She wants us to create both a continuing communication hub that actually does connect and communicate what is working in the world, combined with a new planetary ritual. We've already had Earth Day. This will be our first chance to have a planetary Birth Day."

"The call to action is where TLC can come in," Jane suggested with a sense of excitement. "PSI has focused on how ordinary people can tap their unlimited hidden potential to create a more cooperative and peaceful world. We have all the tools we need, and I sincerely believe that Barbara is correct. We are all intended to be universal humans, and perhaps secretly we always have been."

"I sense this as well," Jack replied. He was pleased that Jane seemed so enthusiastic, and it made him even more excited. "I'm sure the concept of a party celebrating higher awareness is going to appeal to the other TLC members. I'm confident that Hale Dwoskin, Arielle Ford, Marie Diamond, Lynne Twist, Gay Hendricks, John Gray, Lisa Nichols, Martin Rutte, and Marci Shimoff will all definitely support this."

"So December 22, 2012, can be a real celebration of service and tapping our highest potential!" Jane almost cried with joy. "This is exactly what Thomas always dreamed about when he created the original Success Principles Institute courses with me back in 1973. He would be so proud to see PSI be part of this magnificent event. Why, even when Thomas was working with Alexander Everett back at the beginning of Mind Dynamics before he created PSI, he would talk to me about this crazy vision he had one night—of riding a silver motorcycle through space, leading a group of enlightened beings to planet Earth to plant the seeds for creating higher awareness throughout the planet. Perhaps it is all now coming true!"

Jack was dumbfounded and could hardly speak. "Jane, you know my Golden Motorcycle story, don't you?" he finally managed. "How come you never shared Thomas's vision with me until now?"

"I did hear you talk about the Golden Motorcycle Gang at one of the TLC meetings, but I never really made the connection until now," she admitted. "Thomas loved motorcycles and he had his students learn to ride them as part of our PSI trainings."

"I think I know why. Riding a motorcycle requires absolute focus and concentration. Good training for almost any occupation!"

"Oh, for Thomas the lessons went far beyond training for occupations," Jane explained. "He felt that a true appreciation of motorcycles and how to ride them was a metaphor for a true appreciation of *life*. Thomas could demonstrate how everything you need to know to personally develop and succeed in life you could learn from riding and caring for motorcycles. He would start with general insights on integrity, such as, 'You are responsible for where you ride, how you ride, and where you finish.' He would stress a rider's responsibility to others: 'It's irresponsible to be out of control and leave your accidents to be cleaned up by others.'

"Thomas believed that personal development requires measures of honesty and self-awareness: 'The ride you take today is not the ride you took before; you are different every day; make sure you know where you're at physically, emotionally, intellectually, and spiritually.' But for him, riding a motorcycle was no

155

more of a solo exercise than living among people on Earth, and many of the same cautions applied. 'Don't ride with careless riders,' he said. 'You'll eventually get caught up in their carelessness.' Thomas also taught a great deal about the practical side of maintaining motorcycles, from choice of fuel and transmission oil to where on the road it might be safest to ride during a rainstorm."

"I had no idea he was such an avid motorcyclist," Jack commented, still absorbing the remarkable synchronicity that his own connection to motorcycles was mirrored in the teachings developed by Jane's husband while creating PSI. "I've never been a motorcycle hobbyist while here on Earth, but the image of being part of a celestial Golden Motorcycle Gang has stayed with me for decades."

"Well, for Thomas it really was more than just his love of riding motorcycles," Jane responded. "He had more than 100 specific points in his curriculum, and I would be happy to share them with you in writing. He loved riding motorcycles—but even more, he loved using his knowledge of them to teach the fundamental principles of success and happiness."

Jack had always wanted to meet Jane's husband, but due to Thomas's premature death in an airplane accident in 1983, he'd never had the chance. Jack wasn't sure that at the time he would have been bold enough to realize that his memory of the Golden Motorcycle Gang was real or just a thought, and he certainly wouldn't have been ready to hear that Thomas was a member of the original Silver Motorcycle Gang.

Looking at Jane now and seeing so much emotion in her eyes, Jack realized that in some mystical way, both the Golden Motorcycle Gang and the Silver Motorcycle Gang were very real indeed. There was a larger purpose to his life, and he was not alone in working toward the fulfillment of that mission.

If nothing else, he thought, *the December 22, 2012, celebration of a planetary birthing experience of ourselves as universal beings would assemble all members of the Golden and Silver Motorcycle Gangs. Truly, 'the gang's all here.' Everyone just needs to be given a venue and opportunity to come together and shine.*

Turning back to Jane, he said, "Barbara, Bill, and I are meeting here after your video interview tomorrow; and we agree that we would like you to stay for the meeting."

Jack then looked at his wife and gave her a big smile. "Honey, you should join us as well. To pull this off will be a major effort, and your participation will also be essential."

"Count me in," Inga replied joyfully.

Jack lifted his glass of wine, and looking deeply into Jane's and Inga's eyes, joyfully concluded the evening's conversation. "Let us toast Thomas and all those who have come before us with the vision and intent to create a better life for everyone on planet Earth."

"And may Barbara get even more than ten million people to her Birth Day party on December 22, 2012!" added Jane, in the final toast of the evening.

THE RULE OF FIVE

*"Success is the sum of small efforts,
repeated day in and day out."*

— FLORENCE TAYLOR

"Thank you so much, Jane," Bill said, concluding the interview for *Tapping the Source*. "Jack is waiting for us in his conference room with Barbara and Inga."

Jane followed Bill out the door, crossed the walk next to Jack's swimming pool, and entered a beautiful conference room with a billiards table. The coffee table was laden with fruit, soft drinks, and water—along with glasses, plates, and silverware. Barbara, Jack, and Inga were sitting on two large couches; upon seeing Jane, Barbara went over and gave her a hug.

"I have been such an admirer of yours for years," Jane told her warmly. "I've always felt that you were years ahead of the rest of us in seeing the critical issues facing humanity."

"I'm not sure how much Jack has told you, but the vision I have been carrying for the last 45 years is now ripe for manifestation. I'm so grateful that I'm still alive to participate with you all in the Transformational Leadership Council," Barbara answered.

"Well, let's get started," Jack declared. "I asked Inga to help draw up an agenda for today's meeting. Inga, will you lead us through it, please."

"Barbara, after Jack explained what you told him yesterday," Inga began, "I had a better understanding of your metaphor of Birth 2012 and that the celebration needs to mirror what we would do if we were actually giving birth.

"As a mother, I can remember the anxiety I felt before the actual birth of my first child. I also remember how exhausted I was afterward. Without the support of my family and my community of friends, I'm not sure how the baby or I would have survived. My doctor was important—but the nurses and support staff, along with my friends and family, were even more important in the long run. I believe we need to think about all the needs that this birth is going to require and then assign different groups to handle all the anticipated challenges."

"I very much like the way you're thinking, Inga. What is key for me is not just the celebration and the Birth Day, but the ongoing health of the 'child,'" Barbara said with a laugh. "The point of using 2012 as a marker is not just to have a worldwide celebration, but to have people continue to support the vision for years to come. We are talking about the birth of a new consciousness throughout the planet. A one-time celebration is just the beginning, and in the end not significant, unless we find ways for people to connect in ongoing dialogue and activity."

Jane smiled as she joined the conversation. "Now you're talking my language. PSI is all about ongoing dialogue and activity. What's the first step?"

Jack thought for a moment and then observed, "I think we need to start by focusing on how we're going to get ten million or more people to be aware of December 22, 2012, as the Birth Day for a New Earth. I think the key to doing that will be to create a website where we can post updates about who is doing what, where, and when. And based on what I've learned from marketing in my own work, I think creating and posting video clips on the site is going to be essential. We'll need to create a site that is highly interactive, making it easy for anyone on the Internet to post their own chats and videos."

Bill said, "But this is not as easy as it sounds. I have worked with hundreds of authors, and what you're describing is the goal of all of them. In essence, everyone I represent is trying to create an online community around his or her book or topic, but most authors seem to face two problems. First they need to have a cause or purpose that is authentic, and most of them actually do have that. What they don't have is a way to generate traffic to the site at a level that moves the needle."

"I learned a lot about how to do this from the way the movie *The Secret* was promoted, and also from how Mark Victor Hansen and I promoted our *Chicken Soup for the Soul* books," Jack assured him.

"First we have to carefully coordinate everything we do. In the case of *The Secret,* we had most of the members of TLC send out e-mails to their entire mailing lists with a link to a free preview of the film. I think that with all of our combined lists, we reached around 12 million people. By the time those on the lists received their fifth or sixth e-mail on the same day—all from major authors, teachers, and leaders whom they already trusted—they were convinced that it would be worth their time to view the movie's trailer. It was quite a phenomenon. We need to create the same kind of campaign for getting people to the Birth Day–party website, and we need to make sure there is enough compelling information on this site when they arrive there that they will become members of the Birth 2012 movement."

"This is why I knew you were essential to help organize this event, Jack," Barbara responded. "If I am the mother of this event, as many people are calling me, then you are definitely one of its fathers. You have this fatherly energy that not only reassures people, but provides the practical leadership that allows my feminine creativity to become grounded and manifested."

"It's so interesting that you use that metaphor of the mother and father for creating an event like this," Jack said. "When Mark and I launched the *Chicken Soup* books, he was much more the marketer than I was. At first I focused on the creative end, but over time I realized that the marketing side was just as important as the creative side. Mark and I used to comment that we needed the feminine energy to nurture and birth the child, and then the masculine energy to metaphorically raise the child. Writing and editing the books were the creative, feminine side of the equation; while marketing and promoting them were the masculine side.

"Throughout history there have only been a few leaders who combined both the visionary feminine energy with the taking-action masculine energy. For us to be successful, we're going to need to work together to apply both . . . and to be *really* successful, we're going to need to follow what Mark and I call the Rule of Five."

"What is the Rule of Five?" Barbara, Bill, and Jane all asked at once.

"It's something Mark and I developed when we first started to promote our books," Jack stated with excitement. "At the beginning, the original *Chicken Soup for the Soul* book was not selling as rapidly as Mark and I had anticipated. But then we spoke to Brian Tracy, the successful motivational author and business guru, and he explained to us what he calls the 'law of probability.'

"Brian's law of probability states that the more activities you engage in, the higher the probability that you will discover an activity that will have an impact on your goal, disproportionate to the level of effort you expend with any single activity. To put it more simply, the more things you try, the more likely one of them will work.

"Shortly after that lesson, Mark and I decided to consult with Ron Scolastico, a former professor of philosophy who is able to access really deep states of simple but profound wisdom. In our session, Ron explained how even seemingly impossible tasks could be achieved by focused and consistent effort. He told us, 'If you were to go to a tree every day and take just five swings at it with an ax, eventually even the biggest tree in the world would have to come down.'"

Jack paused as his friends absorbed what he shared. "Mark and I thought this was a most useful metaphor and wonderful advice," he continued, "so we decided that every day we would send out five free promotional copies of our book, or we would coordinate five radio interviews, or make five cold calls to major celebrities. Not everything we did worked, but with constant focus and a willingness to experiment with new ideas and do five new things every day, no matter what, we more than achieved our goal of having a number one *New York Times* best-selling book.

"That book, which countless publishers had rejected, went on to sell more than ten million copies in 47 languages. And now there are more than 200 books in the series with more than 500 million copies sold worldwide—all because of what we now call the Rule of Five."

"That's fascinating, but how do we apply this to the promotion of the Birth 2012 celebration?" Jane asked.

"For the Rule of Five to work, you need a clear and focused purpose," Jack explained. "Both Mark and I believed that our real goal was to use the *Chicken Soup for the Soul* books to change the world in a positive way, one story at a time. Of course, we wanted to sell a lot of books, and we enjoyed making a lot of money in the process, but the money and sales were actually secondary goals. I think the same is true for the 2012 Birth Day celebration. Yes, we want to get as many people as possible to create celebrations all across the globe—but even more important, we want to awaken them and start them on their own individual journey of personal transformation."

"I agree," Barbara said. "Although in this instance, the individual journey must mirror and support the larger collective journey."

"Yes, that's definitely the case," Jack agreed. "One of the reasons I'm excited to work with you, Barbara, is that my decades of experience in helping people with individual transformation dovetails so perfectly at this time with your larger vision of global transformation. There is, for perhaps the first time on Earth, an almost exact connection between the individual journey and the global journey for all humanity.

"When Mark and I used the Rule of Five to promote the original *Chicken Soup for the Soul* book, we did some outrageous things that produced amazing results. For example, one day when we couldn't think of what to do, we came up with the idea to send all of the jurors on the O.J. Simpson murder trial a free copy of the book . . . and soon many of the major networks were commenting on this book that the jurors were reading. We even received a nice letter from Judge Ito [who presided over the trial] thanking us for thinking of the jurors."

Jack watched each of his friends smile at this, and then went on. "Another day we bought a copy of *The Celebrity Address Book,* and started sending out copies of *Chicken Soup for the Soul* to actors, producers, and directors in Hollywood just to create some buzz about it. The book was sent to Della Reese and the producer of the hit television show *Touched by an Angel,* and soon the entire cast and crew were given copies by the director, who raved at how the spirit of the book was identical to the feeling that the show was intended to create for viewers. That story was written up in *Variety* magazine and later went out over the Associated Press wire service.

"As you can see, it's going to be important to think outside of the box and come up with promotional ideas that may at first seem unconventional, and many of them will not work. But with persistence and adherence to the Rule of Five, we will definitely be successful."

"I'm beginning to see how this all comes together," Jane remarked. "For me, the way you explain the Rule of Five is how I describe for my students the impact of positive action. Every positive action is like dropping a stone into a pond. At first you have no idea where the ripples from each action may take you.

"I see that if everyone involved makes the commitment to take five positive steps a day, even a project as large as this can be easily achieved. The key will be to create a core action team that is promoting the Birth 2012 event on a daily basis, in ways both big and small. We don't need a large budget to do this. I'm sure that college students and even high-school students throughout the world will want to volunteer to be part of such an inspiring—and as my grandchildren say, 'awesome'—event."

"Yes," Jack agreed. "Once we enroll a large volunteer group, we can coordinate with our colleagues who are creating similar events for the Pachamama Alliance, Four Years. Go., the Bioneers, the Institute of HeartMath, the Club of Budapest, the Institute of Noetic Sciences, the Shift Network, and anyone else who shares the basic belief in 2012 as the birth of a New Earth."

"I'm so glad to hear that you're already thinking about including other groups," Barbara added. "It's important that people understand that this is not a Barbara Marx Hubbard idea or event; it's a *world* event. I am but one voice of many that are coming together to bring this awareness to as many individuals as possible at this time."

"Yes, but you are a key player in all of this, Barbara," Bill affirmed. "I have known you for almost 20 years now, and you have been clear with this message of humanity's new story and the birth of universal humans even before I met you."

"Yes, I am a clear voice," Barbara confirmed. "But do not be mistaken. An event of this magnitude cannot happen without the participation of hundreds of other leaders, and thousands if not tens of thousands of volunteers."

"I can see that we're just getting started here," Jane said. "I have a plane to catch, so I'm going to have to leave, but I don't see any obstacles to achieving Barbara's vision of having millions of people gather to celebrate the New Earth and the new story of humanity.

This dream is one that so many of us have had for so many years. We've often expressed it in many different ways, but I agree with all of you that we are living in a special historical moment, and that we must do something extraordinary to commemorate the event. As my stepson, who has just discovered the card game of Texas Hold'em, says, 'I'm all in!'"

"That goes for me, too," Bill promised. Turning to Jane, he told her, "I was planning to take you to the airport, so I think we should break for now. I have a sense that Barbara and Jack will have assignments for us soon enough."

"You can definitely count on that," was Jack's final comment as the group stood up and hugged each other before leaving.

The first steps had been taken, and Jack felt aligned with his destiny chosen so many years ago when riding his golden motorcycle throughout the universe.

Chapter
19

THE DIAMOND
MOTORCYCLE
GANG

*"What cannot be achieved in one lifetime will
happen when one lifetime is joined to another."*

— RABBI HAROLD KUSHNER

Jack woke up the next morning full of energy and
enthusiasm for life. He completed his daily practice of
light yoga exercises, followed by a brief meditation. He
chose to meditate in the garden, surrounded by the
fresh scent of jasmine, gardenias, and a variety of roses.
His meditation that morning brought him to a deep
trancelike state that seemed almost like a dream. . . .

He found himself looking into the sky, and saw an incredible diamond motorcycle rider racing toward him. Soon he saw two more riders behind the first, then three more behind those two, then five behind those three, and then seven behind those five. The sequence continued, almost like a divine diamond flock of geese revving their engines and flying toward him until the entire sky was filled with diamond motorcycles. There must have been thousands of them filling the sky; and each was occupied by a young, smiling man or woman who exuded health and strength and a palpable aura of well-being.

Suddenly, the lead rider, a female of astonishing strength, grace, and beauty, did something akin to a "sky wheelie" and came floating to a halt no more than five feet away from Jack's face. The first words out her mouth were: "Thank you, Jack."

It was really more of a thought than actual words, and Jack was taken aback. "Thank me for what?" was all he could think back.

"Why, for holding the space for the Diamond Motorcycle Gang to get ready for the next level of human evolution, of course. You've become something of a legend back at the Academy of Enlightenment. Our teachers have been following your progress ever since you decided to incarnate as a human being.

Everyone is very proud of you and your fellow members of the Golden Motorcycle Gang.

"Your *Chicken Soup* series has warmed and nourished the souls of millions of people. The books have expanded human beings' appreciation of the necessity of compassion and of an understanding of the nobility of 'regular' people's existences, the surprising inherent inclusiveness of the human experience. Every book in the series points to the truth that no matter who you are—a famous celebrity, a billionaire CEO, a housewife, or a hardworking soul living paycheck to paycheck—there is dignity in everyone. You've pointed to the truth that humans define themselves by their relationships to others, and they do so in ways as diverse, plentiful, and creative as anything a van Gogh, a Beethoven, or a Shakespeare can imagine."

Jack managed to collect himself and replied, "I am humbled by your words. Yet I'm just one part of the great collective of authors and contributors to the series, and we could never have made the impact we have without their guidance and leadership."

"We know this to be true," the lead rider said. "The diversity of the community of writers and contributors is a vital element of the series, which gives it its strength, the secret ingredient to the *Chicken Soup*. The books have given so many people the chance to share their experiences and challenges, and with that have not only helped the readers of each book, but established a true community—and you shouldn't think that communal sense ends when the book is put back on the shelves.

"Indeed, as you are learning right now, this communal sense is at the core of what you and your friends and colleagues, especially those who form the Transformational Leadership Council, are being called upon to accomplish for your planet in the next several years. Through TLC and other organizations, the Golden Motorcycle Gang has laid a wonderful foundation for redefining the meaning of success. I believe it was one of your TLC members who suggested that in the 21st century the goal is to be 'go-givers' rather than 'go-getters.'

"Jack, your ability, through your Success Principles training, to reach and train transformational leaders in almost every country in the world no matter how remote is a remarkable achievement. For the first time on planet Earth, people are beginning to realize that true success means fulfilling the purpose of one's soul and not just serving the immediate goals of one's ego. None of this would be happening were it not for your efforts and those of the other members of both the Golden and Silver Motorcycle Gangs.

174

"Now we, the members of the Diamond Motorcycle Gang, are ready to incarnate and take humanity to the next level. Some of us are already in human form. And none of us would have had the courage to take on the human challenges that lay before us had it not been for your commitment—and, frankly, your initial success in waking up so many human beings to the potential they already carry to become true universal humans."

Jack noted that the words/thoughts from the Diamond Motorcycle leader emanated clarity and kindness. He found himself telling her, "Well, sometimes I have actually felt discouraged about the progress we have made during my lifetime on Earth. Do you really think we've made such a difference?"

"As a human being, it is hard to feel the energy and understand how much the world has changed in the 67 years since you arrived," she explained. "Outwardly, there are still signs of struggle and hardship for the seven billion human beings on planet Earth, but energetically the world has definitely changed. There is greater awareness, a greater sense of compassion, and a greater sense of connection among all humans. It will still take many years to eliminate most of the earthly conflicts—but rest assured, with the changes you and the rest of the Golden and Silver Motorcycle

Gangs have initiated, it is only a matter of time before there truly will be what many have called the Golden Age, or the age of 'Heaven on Earth.'"

The leader revved her motorcycle engine to keep from coming to a complete standstill. "We just wanted to visit with you during your meditation to assure you that what you are contemplating doing with Barbara, Jane, and hundreds of others—to organize this grand Birth Day celebration for December 22, 2012—is well worth doing," she assured him. "Your success is guaranteed with or without this celebration, but the celebration itself will enhance and speed up the transition to a world of higher awareness for all.

"Even those who don't participate will be impacted by the energetic change of such a vast and focused intentional event. And, of course, we are here to thank you so that you may take our message of gratitude to all who have helped you (and will help you in the future) create a more peaceful, cooperative, and harmonious environment on planet Earth.

"What happens on Earth is important for life throughout the universe. Earth is a test case for the potential of free will in action. It was no accident that you saw this small distressed planet as you rode on your Golden Motorcycle so many years ago on solstice break."

Jack was literally speechless, caught between his awareness of himself as Jack the human being, and Jack the luminous being whose compassion had brought him to Earth and to the life of a writer and teacher for so many millions.

Before he could utter or even think the thought of "Thank you," the leader of the Diamond Motorcycle Gang revved up her engine once again and made a sharp turn in the air toward the rising sun in the east. The rest of the riders, still in formation, followed their leader. But just before departing, she turned and winked at Jack and sent him her final thought, "By the way, the unanimous decision at the Academy was to give you an *A* for both effort and results. You are going to graduate with highest honors when you return. Congratulations."

And then they were gone in a blaze of shining, glorious light, which sparkled off each diamond motorcycle as far as Jack's eye could see. . . .

Jack was in a state of profound bliss when he awoke from his trance. He went back into the house, where Inga was preparing her morning coffee, and gave her a kiss on the lips. He smiled at her startled but pleased face and lovingly told her, "This is going to be a very good day."

AFTERWORD

Calling All Agents for
Conscious Evolution

*"I cannot do all the good that the world needs,
but the world needs all the good that I can do."*

— JANA STANFIELD

It is not an accident that you picked up this book.
The story of the Golden Motorcycle Gang touches all
who believe that there is a higher purpose to their existence and that they are part of a group destined to

work together to create a better planet. There are almost seven billion people living on planet Earth, and no one person or single group can provide the guidance, leadership, and resources to ensure what Barbara Marx Hubbard and other visionaries and scientists refer to as "Conscious Evolution."

Jack, Barbara, Bill, and those who are part of the story of the Golden Motorcycle Gang don't believe that they have all the answers to the world's problems, or that they are in any way superior to the tens of millions of other people already actively working to create the best possible conditions on Earth for all human beings and other species of life. They are willing, however, to take a stand for what they believe in and to welcome others to work with them.

The world is facing multiple crises. As authors, we are calling upon you, our readers, to become Agents for Conscious Evolution. What that means in terms of expression will be different for each and every one of you. What you need to know is that each of you is essential to ensure that life on this planet evolves in a positive direction. We invite you to focus on what is going well in your immediate world and to overcome the fear and inertia that grips all of us from time to time.

No one is a perfect human being. In telling the story of Jack Canfield's life from birth to the present day, we wanted to show that even for someone who achieves unimaginable success in life, there are constant challenges. Jack was blessed to have the vision of the Golden Motorcycle Gang as a young person in graduate school. That vision helped him stay true to his higher purpose. Barbara Marx Hubbard had a similar vision—and so did Thomas Willhite, Stewart Emery, and so many others who influenced Jack's life. Our hope is that you stay true to *your* higher purpose as well.

If you're looking for a way to identify or express your higher purpose, we encourage you to visit these websites: **www.shiftmovement.com**, **www.barbaramarx hubbard.com**, **www.tappingthesourcemovie.com**, **www.birth2012.com**, **www.goldenmotorcyclegang .com**, and **www.jackcanfield.com**. Here, you will find resources that you can use to explore maximizing your experiences in both your inner and outer worlds. We believe that both are equally important to living a balanced life and to making a sustainable difference.

You need to know who you really are, and you need to go within in order to be certain that you have your own internal house in order. And like any house, your internal psyche may need constant cleaning up.

However, once your inner house is in good shape, you need to explore how you can interact with others in the outer world to put your values, convictions, and inner guidance to work.

Our good friend and fellow Transformational Leadership Council member Marci Shimoff has stated eloquently that one of the most important decisions you can make is to be happy. Marci has written the bestseller *Happy for No Reason* and speaks frequently on the topic of happiness. To that end, in the film *Tapping the Source,* she relates the wonderful Chinese proverb that shows the direct link between happiness in your soul and happiness first in your family, then your community, then your nation, and then the entire world. According to Marci, there is nothing more important for contributing to world peace and happiness than focusing on your individual peace and happiness. What is special about these times and the concept of Conscious Evolution is that for the first time on planet Earth, we are conscious of how our own behavior and emotions can significantly impact others in specific and practical ways.

Jack Canfield has spent his entire life helping people discover tools and techniques that will make them more aware, more joyous, and more successful in everything they do. Thanks to the insights from Barbara

Marx Hubbard and others, we now see that these tools and techniques serve an even higher purpose than creating individual and collective happiness. That higher purpose is to serve as an agent for evolutionary change. For those of you connected with traditional religious organizations, you can think of evolutionary change as that which is aligned with your spiritual purpose; change that puts you in closer proximity to your God and the highest expression of divinity in all areas of life.

It takes work to change this world. Do not be fooled by those who say the world will take care of itself. It won't. Our scientists have studied the nature of systems, and our present-day systems—whether in terms of ecology, economics, business, government, education, or health—are literally breaking down. Ignoring these breakdowns can only lead to entropy and the destruction of our planet. It is not too late for change, and just as with any task, the first steps need not be large. Each of us has a unique gift and a unique set of talents. We are here to use them.

We encourage you to review the five questions that Barbara Marx Hubbard was given in 2003:

1. What do you know of the original plan?

2. Do you have any memory of having volunteered to be of service to Earth at this particular time?

3. If so, do you remember your contract?

4. What do you do best in the world that only you can do?

5. What are you to do now, and what tools or resources do you need to do it?

It is not essential that you answer yes to the first three questions. If you do happen to remember your original contract and specifically why you came to Earth, that is wonderful and a clear sign that you're part of the Golden, Silver, or Diamond Motorcycle Gangs. However, the truly important questions are the last two: *What do you do best in the world that only you can do?* and *What are you to do now, and what tools or resources do you need to do it?*

It may be that at this specific moment in time, your unique gift and purpose is to raise your children as conscious loving human beings or to coach a Little League team, give piano lessons, work with senior citizens, be a hospice aid, or volunteer in an animal shelter. It may be that you are motivated to find solutions for housing the homeless, ending violence, creating sustainable ecology, ending world hunger, enhancing political freedom, fostering peace, ending sexual slavery, or empowering the disenfranchised. Of course, if you have a skill set that includes the ability to communicate the message of the Golden Motorcycle Gang and Conscious Evolution to large groups of people, that asset is excellent as well.

What is ultimately important is that you make the effort to consciously be the best person you can be, and to allow yourself to dream your greatest dream. If you're able to sense that you really are connected on the deepest level to all other human beings, animals, and plants on this Earth, you can use that perception to make a difference.

We cannot specify or predict exactly what you will do or how you will do it. We just invite you to step up and participate. The world needs all you can give.

We invite you to stay connected and to use the websites mentioned in the appendices of this book to share your own unique messages with others. We welcome your posts, your video clips, and any messages that have positive value for yourself and others. If you have a solution that is working in your own community, share it with the world through these websites. Make them your own, for no matter who you are or how great or limited your resources, you can make—and *are* making—a difference in the world. Just be sure that the difference you make is the most positive and powerful difference possible.

We thank you for reading our little book and sharing it with others. Most of all we thank you for joining us on the journey of self-discovery, which will enable all of us to work together to choose an evolutionary path that honors our ancestors and their sacrifices, and that is worthy of future generations waiting to be born.

As you reflect on what your life purpose is and how you want to spend your time on planet Earth, remember that your imagination may be your most important asset. The only limits to your future achievements and contributions are those you set yourself. You were presented with this book because you were meant to read it. The fact that you *have* read it is meaningful, not just for you, but for others you meet and with whom you will share your new insights and knowledge.

You now have a wonderful opportunity to come join Jack and the others on their ride. We cannot predict what this will mean for you, but we hope it will create that same feeling of joy and liberation that Jack experienced so many years ago when he was riding his golden motorcycle throughout the universe!

APPENDIX A

Action Steps for Agents of Conscious Evolution (ACE)

"We must be willing to let go of the life we planned so as to have the life that is waiting for us."

— E. M. FORSTER

"Don't be satisfied with the stories that come before you. Unfold your own myth."

— JALAL AL-DIN RUMI

To learn more about the concept of Conscious Evolution, we encourage you to visit the following websites:

- **www.goldenmotorcyclegang.com**
- **www.barbaramarxhubbard.com**
- **www.shiftmovement.com**
- **www.birth2012.com**

All of these sites contain information about what it means to be an agent for Conscious Evolution; they'll also enable you to connect with courses, groups, and activities that can help you fulfill your own higher purpose.

For those of you motivated to become *active* agents for Conscious Evolution, we strongly recommend attending ACE training workshops. The basic curricula, like Conscious Evolution itself, continues to evolve—but below is a brief description of the initial core 12-week course that was developed by Barbara Marx Hubbard and Stephen Dinan of the Shift Network.

For those of you reading this book prior to December 22, 2012, you can use this information to participate in the events being scheduled to celebrate day one of the New Earth. For those of you reading in 2013 and beyond, you can use this information to connect with the ongoing focus groups and networks dedicated to bringing the message of Conscious Evolution to millions of people throughout the world, sharing "what is working" with others.

ACE Training provides three primary competencies:

1. A comprehensive understanding of the core concepts of Conscious Evolution

2. Practices to apply Conscious Evolution to your own life

3. Skills in facilitating and leading transformative processes for creating group coherence

Class topics include:

- Communicating the Sacred Story of Conscious Evolution

- Choosing to Evolve

- Practicing Evolutionary Spirituality

- Making the Shift from Ego to Essence

- Becoming a Catalyst for Social Evolution by Following Your Compass of Joy

- Forming a Resonant Field with Pioneering Souls
- Discovering the Patterns of a Co-creative Society
- Pioneering Synergistic Democracy
- Tracking, Connecting, and Communicating What's Working
- Participating in Birth 2012
- Beyond 2012: Becoming a Universal Human and Setting the Evolutionary Agenda
- Celebrating the Journey

To find out more about the course, go to: **http://theacetraining.com/ACE.**

APPENDIX B

New Beginnings

December 21 and 22, 2012, represent a time for new beginnings. Many organizations are preparing major events for either or both of those days. In *The Golden Motorcycle Gang,* we have featured the activities being organized by Barbara Marx Hubbard's Foundation for Conscious Evolution and by the Shift Network. Yet there are many other organizations also creating wonderful events. For example:

— Under the leadership of Daniel Pinchbeck, Alex Theory, Violaine Corradi, and Richard Lukens, Unify Earth (**www.unifyearth.com**) has created a network of networks to ensure that ongoing solutions are shared with organizations throughout the world.

— The *New York Times* bestselling author of *The Four Agreements,* don Miguel Ruiz, is inviting each and every one of us to join him in making the end of the Mayan calendar a moment of positive change for humanity. He is asking us to make an agreement that this will be the end of humans living in fear and superstition, and instead the beginning of a new era based in truth, integrity, love, and awareness. Throughout 2012, don Miguel Ruiz will focus on planting this seed of awareness. For more information and updates, please visit: **wwwmiguelruiz.com**.

— Led by Brent Hunter, the Rainbow Bridge (**http://therainbowbridge.tv**) is, in his words, "a book and movement created to help unify humanity and to create a bridge to a positive and peaceful future in the 21st century . . . by using universal principles found within the world's major religions."

— Push4Peace (**http://push4peace.org**) is an organization that hopes to get one billion people focused on peace initiatives throughout the world.

Doubtless there will be many similar efforts from thousands of other organizations. We encourage you to find whichever one you most resonate with and contribute your unique talents and perspective to the events and campaigns that are designed to provide meaningful support throughout the 21st century.

If you are reading this book prior to December 21/22, 2012, you will enjoy participating in the events being created for celebrating this dramatic window in time that comes only once every 26,000 years. There will be major shows, webcasts, live television events, Twitter and Facebook happenings, video games, flash mobs, mobile apps, YouTube webisodes, podcasts, and every type of celebration imaginable throughout these two days.

Since this book goes to the printer well before the finalization of plans for the major Earth Birth celebrations on December 21 and 22, 2012, we offer just one of the possible scenarios already in the works from the Shift Network and the Foundation for Conscious Evolution for what such celebrations are likely to include.

Imagine the Day

This preliminary scenario for the December 22, 2012, celebration has been provided by members of the Shift Network. This is an edited version of evolving plans.

BIRTH 2012
CO-CREATING A PLANETARY SHIFT

A GLOBAL CELEBRATION OF CONSCIOUSNESS, COMMUNITY, CREATIVITY, AND COLLABORATION

"Tell me and I will forget. Show me and I will remember. Involve me and I will understand."

— CONFUCIUS

Mission

To facilitate the highest level of planetary coherence that has happened on a single day. By offering powerful experiences of collective focus and diverse celebrations of community, creativity, and global collaboration, we hope to shift and awaken individual and global consciousness to birth a universal humanity.

Goal

Engaging a global audience throughout 24 hours of art, activism, music, intention, celebration, recognition, and respect for all humanity. This will empower the shift to a more aware, peaceful, sustainable, healthy, and prosperous world.

Target Demographic

The goal is to reach an audience of over 100 million people spanning age, ethnicity, gender, socioeconomics, and religious groups from every country in the world.

Experience Overview

On December 22, 2012, citizens around the world will experience a day of conscious action, intention, celebration, and renewal.

Sample day:

<u>8 A.M.: Prayer and Meditation</u>

Suggested Meditation on the Planetary Birth (MUSIC AND TONING IS HEARD):

Place yourself in the universe, like the astronauts did.

Feel the ecstatic joy of floating weightless in space, seeing your planet as one living body.

Sense the reality of the New Earth now awakening to itself as a whole planetary being.

As a universal human, now see yourself within the planetary body as it struggles to take its first coordinated breath to bring nourishment to all its members.

Feel millions of people like yourself, desiring to be more, to give more, to care for each other and Earth life.

The time of our collective awakening is at hand. The hour of our "planetary birth" has come.

Open your inner eyes and sense the Light, the Impulse of Creation that for billions of years has brought all beings from No Thing at All to Everything That Is.

Hear the tone of resonance that aligns us. Imagine everything that works connecting and coordinating. We can feed, house, and clothe ourselves. We can make it through together.

Smile your first planetary smile.

We are one. We are good. We are whole. We are born.

Now ask yourself: What is my gift to the cosmic child, humanity? What am I called to do right now to assist in this birthing process? What do I need to do it?

*Write your answers and send to Shift Network at: **www.Birth2012.com**.*

9:30 A.M.–9:45 A.M.: Chant Around the World

Beginning on Christmas Island, Kiritimati, citizens will engage in a roaming CHANT that will travel the world. The CHANT will be held in 15-minute increments and will be passed through time zones.

9:45 A.M–11:15 A.M.: Yoga and Other Forms of Conscious Movement (such as Tai Chi, Qigong, Etc).

Yoga studios and teachers will join Birth 2012 by hosting a class at a designated time with the intention being set by all students for global unity, peace, sustainability, and compassion. Studios can choose to donate a portion of the proceeds to a charity of their choice.

10:00 A.M.–12:00 P.M.: Global Broadcast

In movie theaters, on the web, and on big screens in major city centers (such as New York's Times Square), the Shift Network presents the broadcast of Birth 2012. Elements of the broadcast may include, but are not limited to:

- Children's Choir—one child from every country in the world

- The story of how we got here, from the big bang until today

- State of the World address

- Vision of where we are going and what we can do together

12:00 P.M.: Time of Service

We will ask communities and organizations to submit their highest needs to the website prior to the event. Participants will volunteer with organizations from 12:00 P.M.–3:00 P.M.

1:30 P.M.: Flash Mobs

The Birth 2012 flash mobs will focus on creating community.

3:00 P.M.–5:00 P.M.: Coherence-Building Experiences

5:00 P.M.–6:00 P.M.: Drumming, Kirtan, Dance, Spoken Word

A call to artists, activists, and musicians to find public venues in which to perform their craft.

6:00 P.M.: Fire Ceremony—a Pledge to Global Citizenry

7:00 P.M.: Globally Local Dinners or Feasts for the World

Each participant will be asked to bring food for those less fortunate. Feasts can conclude with cakes and the Birth 2012 candle ceremony.

8:30 P.M.: Music, Dance

11:59 P.M.: Closing Ritual

APPENDIX C

The Transformational Leadership Council Membership List

As you have read in this book, the Transformational Leadership Council (TLC) was created by Jack Canfield as a way to gather leading owners of transformational training, coaching, and media companies—along with transformational thought leaders—in a single association. Many of the members of TLC offer ongoing training, workshops, coaching, and consulting, which will enable you and your organization to continue on your journey of self exploration.

We encourage you to go to the websites listed with each member to find out more about them and their work and connect with any whose programs and projects might be exactly what you need to facilitate your own evolution at this moment in your life.

Raymond	Aaron	www.monthlymentor.com
Arjuna	Ardagh	www.awakeningcoachingtraining.com
Alison	Armstrong	www.understandmen.com
Will	Arntz	
Chris	Attwood	www.enlightenedalliances.com
Janet	Attwood	www.thepassiontest.com
Patty	Aubery	www.chickensoupforthesoul.com
Barnet	Bain	www.barnetbain.com
Anat	Baniel	www.anatbanielmethod.com
Blaine	Bartlett	www.avatar-resources.com
Bill	Bauman	www.billbauman.net
Michael	Beckwith	www.agapelive.com
Rickie	Beckwith	www.apagelive.com
Pete	Bissonette	www.learningstrategies.com
Ray	Blanchard	www.rayblanchard.com
Nicole	Brandon	www.nicolebrandonworldwide.com
Lee	Brower	www.empoweredwealth.com

David	Buck	www.coachville.com
Jim	Bunch	www.jimbunch.com
Inga	Canfield	
Jack	Canfield	www.jackcanfield.com
Sonia	Choquette	www.soniachoquette.com
John	Chupka	www.forgivenesscenter.org
Joyce	Chupka	
Cherie	Clark	www.socialsynergistics.com
Scott	Coady	www.embodiedwisdom.com
DC	Cordova	www.excellerated.com
Stephen M.R.	Covey	www.coveylink.com
Sydney	Cresci	www.makeachangejourneys.com
Steve	D'Annunzio	www.theprosperityparadigm.com
Katie	Darling	www.infinitewave.org
Sandy	Davis	www.resilienceworks.com
John	Dealey	www.smileworld.com
Zen	DeBrucke	www.smartsoulacademy.com
John	Demartini	www.drdemartini.com
Scott	deMoulin	www.scottdemoulin.com
Bobbi	DePorter	www.qln.com
Marie	Diamond	www.mariediamond.com
Stephen	Dinan	www.theshiftnetwork.com
Mike	Dooley	www.tut.com
Ken	Druck	www.jennadruckcenter.org
Joanne	Dunleavy	www.newagreementscoaching.com
Hale	Dwoskin	www.sedona.com
Peter	Einstein	www.ecoactiveamerica.com

Dave	Ellis	www.fallingawake.com
Joan	Emery	www.belvedereconsultants.com
Stewart	Emery	www.belvedereconsultants.com
Roxanne	Emmerich	www.roxanneemmerich.com
Cheryl	Esposito	www.alexsaconsulting.com
Rob	Evans	www.robevans.org
Arielle	Ford	www.arielleford.com
Mike	Foster	www.fosterinstitute.com
Bill	Galt	
John	Gray	www.marsvenus.com
Robert	Guralnick	
Deirdre	Hade	www.deirdrehade.com
Roger	Hamilton	www.resultsfoundation.com
Jim	Hardt	www.biocybernaut.com
Gay	Hendricks	www.hendricks.com
Christine	Hibbard	www.christinehibbard.org
Raz	Ingrasci	www.hoffmaninstitute.org
Lise	Janelle	www.centreforheartliving.com
Fred	Johnson	www.frejon.org
Stephen	Josephs	www.leadershipagility.com
Cynthia	Kersey	www.unstoppable.net
Morty	Lefkoe	www.recreateyourlife.com
Shelly	Lefkoe	www.parentingthelefkoeway.com
Chunyi	Lin	www.springforestqigong.com
Willson	Lin	www.doers.cn
Greg	Link	www.coveylink.com

Robert	MacPhee	www.manifestingfornongurus.com
Jeddah	Mali	www.jeddahmali.com
Fabrizio	Mancini	www.parkercc.edu
Alex	Mandossian	www.alexmandossian.com
Rick	Mars	rlmars@att.net
Howard	Martin	www.heartmath.com
Marcia	Martin	www.1degree-media.com
Scott	Martineau	www.consciousone.com
Tom	McCarthy	www.tommccarthy.com
Peggy	McColl	www.destinies.com
Mark	McKergow	www.sfwork.com
Corinne	McLaughlin	www.visionarylead.org
Lynne	McTaggart	www.lynnemctaggart.com www.thebond.net
Enrico	Melson	www.iamthejourney.com
Ivan	Misner	www.bni.com
Dianne	Morrison	www.morrisonmcnabb.com
Mary	Morrissey	www.marymorrissey.com
Sue	Morter	www.suemorter.com
Lisa	Nichols	www.lisa-nichols.com
Gabriel	Nossovitch	www.gabrielnossovitch.com
Nick	Ortner	www.thetappingsolution.com
Steve	Pavlina	www.stevepavlina.com
John	Perkins	www.johnperkins.org
James	Redmond	www.dynamicvideos.net
Neal	Rogin	www.awakeninguniverse.com
Genpo	Roshi	http://bigmind.org

Deborah	Rozman	www.quantumintech.com
Martin	Rutte	www.martinrutte.com
Nancy	Salzman	www.nxivm.com
Paul	Scheele	www.learningstrategies.com
Robert	Scheinfeld	www.bobscheinfeld.com
James	Selman	www.paracomm.com
Marci	Shimoff	www.happyfornoreason.com
Yakov	Smirnoff	www.yakov.com
Donna	Steinhorn	www.coachingtosuccess.com
Guy	Stickney	
Orjan	Strindlund	www.coachpower.se
Terry	Tillman	www.227company.com
Lynne	Twist	www.soulofmoney.org
Nina	Utne	www.utne.com
Joe	Vitale	www.mrfire.com
Matt	Weinstein	www.playfair.com
Maggie	Weiss	www.pacificedge.us
Marcia	Wieder	www.dreamuniversity.com
Jane (JC)	Willhite	www.psiseminars.com
Marianne	Williamson	www.marianne.com
Mikki	Willis	www.mikkiwillis.com
Stephanie	Wolfswinkel	www.sportsmind.com
David	Wood	www.solutionbox.com
David	Wood	www.davidtraining.com
Sandra	Yancey	www.ewomennetwork.com
Tyson	Young	

APPENDIX D

List of Additional Organizations and Their Primary Members

Here is a list of additional organizations (and their primary members) that have influenced the concepts of Transformational Experiential Training and Conscious Evolution.

Evolutionary Leaders

This group of well-known authors, teachers, scientists, social entrepreneurs, business experts, spiritual leaders, journalists, and educators was first convened by Deepak Chopra, President of the Chopra Center; Diane Williams, President of the Source of Synergy Foundation; and Barbara Fields, Executive Director of the Association for Global New Thought; on July 26, 2008, at the Chopra Center in Carlsbad, California.

All members are dedicated to be in service to Conscious Evolution, and the group meets once a year or as appropriate to support projects that have a direct impact on the collective experience of Conscious Evolution, particularly those that allow individuals throughout the world to participate in co-creating the future through live and virtual events.

Website: **www.evolutionaryleaders.net**

Don Beck	Ashok Gangadean	Nina Meyerhof
Michael Bernard Beckwith	Kathleen Gardarian	Deborah Moldow
Joan Borysenko	Tom Gegax	James O'Dea
Gregg Braden	Mark Gerzon	Carter Phipps
Patrick Brauckmann	Charles Gibbs	Carolyn Rangel
Rinaldo Brutoco	Craig Hamilton	Ocean Robbins
Jack Canfield	Kathy Hearn	Rustum Roy
Scott Carlin	Brian Hilliard	Peter Russell
Deepak Chopra	Jean Houston	Elisabet Sahtouris

Mallika Chopra	Barbara Marx Hubbard	Nipun Mehta
Andrew Cohen	Van Jones	Yuka Saionji
Dale Colton	Ervin Laszlo	Gerard Senehi
Wendy Craig-Purcell	Bruce Lipton	Christian Sorensen
Stephen Dinan	Howard Martin	Emily Squires
Gordon Dveirin	Judy Martin	Brian Swimme
Duane Elgin	Fred Matser	Katherine Woodward Thomas
Barbara Fields	Rod McGrew	Lynne Twist
Arielle Ford	Steve McIntosh	Diane Williams
Debbie Ford	Lynne McTaggart	Tom Zender

IONS

The Institute of Noetic Sciences was founded in 1973 by Apollo 14 astronaut Edgar Mitchell with the mission to support individual and collective transformation through consciousness research and educational outreach. "Noetic" comes from the Greek word *nous,* which means "intuitive mind" or "inner knowing." The current president and CEO is Marilyn Mandala Schlitz.

Website: **www.noetic.org**

EarthRise at IONS (a retreat center)
101 San Antonio Road
Petaluma, CA 94952

Carole Angermeir	Stacey Lawson	Belvie Rooks
Peter Baumann	Lou Leeburg	Robert L. Schwartz
Richard Bishop	Walter Link	William "Bill" Sechrest
Charles Brush	Lee Lipsenthal	Fred Segal
Harriot Crosby	Dorothy Lyddon	Diane Temple
John Fetzer	Martha Lyddon	Paul N. Temple
Winston Franklin	Tamas Makray	Lynn Twist
Ann Frost	Austin Marx	Ian Watson
Elizabeth "Betsy" Gordon	Susan Mersereau	Victoria Watson
Willis W. Harman	Edgar D. Mitchell	Rose Welch
Elda Hartley	Lynn Montei	Judith Skutch Whitson
Sandra Hobson	Brendan O'Regan	William W. Whitson
Jim Jensen	Bruce Roberts	Sandra S. Wright
Nan Johnson	Henry J. Rolfs	George Zimmer
	Zoe Rolfs	

Esalen Institute

Esalen Institute is located in the heart of Big Sur, California, and has provided pioneering workshops to more than 300,000 people over the last five decades. Esalen has focused on events and trainings that encourage exploring new possibilities and creating states of higher awareness. Amid the beauty and grandeur of 27 acres of mountain, canyon, and ocean vistas, Esalen Institute is an environment in which true magic can occur.

Website: **www.esalen.org**

Esalen Institute
55000 Highway 1
Big Sur, CA 93920

Bill James	David Lustig	Michael Murphy
Mary Ellen Klee	Tricia McEntee	Gordon Wheeler
Nancy Lunney-Wheeler	Anisa Mehdi	Sam Yau

Omega Institute

Founded in 1977, Omega Institute for Holistic Studies is one of the nation's most trusted sources for wellness and personal growth. With a primary campus located on 195 acres in Rhinebeck, New York, in the beautiful Hudson Valley—as well as other locations around the world—Omega welcomes tens of thousands of people to its workshops, conferences, and retreats. Omega's mission is to provide innovative educational experiences that awaken the best in the human spirit, providing hope and healing for individuals and society.

Website: **http://eomega.org**

Omega Institute
150 Lake Drive
Rhinebeck, NY 12572

Patty Goodwin	Sheryl Lamb	Renee Martin-Nagle
Nigol Koulajian	Elizabeth Lesser	David Orlinsky
Gary Krauthamer	Walter Link	Stephan Rechtschaffen

The Pachamama Alliance

Pachamama is an indigenous Kichwa word meaning "Mother Earth"—or, more completely, "the Earth, the sky, the universe, and all time."

Mission

The Pachamama Alliance's mission is to empower indigenous people of the Amazon rain forest to preserve their lands and culture; and, using insights gained from that work, to educate and inspire individuals everywhere to bring forth a thriving, just, and sustainable world.

To learn more about the organization's work in South America, please visit the website of their sister organization, Fundación Pachamama: **http://pachamama.org.ec**.

Legal and Collective Rights

The Pachamama Alliance provides legal services and makes available training and consulting on indigenous people's collective and legal rights under local, national, and international law.

Website: **http://www.pachamama.org**

The Pachamama Alliance Office
The Presidio Bldg. 1009, Second Floor
P.O. Box 29191
San Francisco, CA 94129

John Perkins, Founder	Bill Twist, Founder	Lynne Twist, Founder

Four Years. Go.

Four Years. Go. is a communication and commitment campaign to create the collective will that is needed to shift the course of history so that by the end of 2014, humanity is on the pathway to a thriving, just, sustainable future for all.

Four Years. Go. intends to reach one billion people in four years and have 200 million of them "take a stand" for a thriving, just, and sustainable way of life— with a minimum of 150 million people taking measurable action to fulfill that stand. The campaign will be conducted by internet connections, social media, and traditional advertising and organizing.

Four Years. Go. was initiated by the Pachamama Alliance in collaboration with the advertising network of Wieden + Kennedy. It immediately attracted partners and allies from many sectors. The original circle of creators include Bill and Lynne Twist, Jon Love, Dan Wieden, and Mark Dubois.

Over 1,300 organizations have already signed up as allies, including Earth Day and the Sierra Club.

Website: **www.fouryearsgo.org**

Video on YouTube:
www.youtube.com/watch?v=B_6iTCo5Ci8

Jack Canfield's early support message:
www.youtube.com/watch?v=nTCR5LkGh8A

Institute of HeartMath

The Institute of HeartMath is a research and educational organization dedicated to creating tools that allow individuals to reduce stress, self-regulate emotions, and increase energy and resilience in order to live healthier, more productive, and happier lives. The vision and quest for global coherence is the primary present and future mission of HeartMath.

Website: **www.hearthmath.org**

Institute of HeartMath
14700 West Park Ave.
Boulder Creek, CA 95006

Doc Childre, Founder	Brian Kabaker	Sandra "Sandy" Royall
Katherine Floriano	Donna Koontz	Deborah Rozman
Hobart S. Johnson	Howard Martin	Claire Shafe
	Toni Roberts	

The Shift Network

The Shift Network is dedicated to empowering an evolutionary shift of consciousness that will lead to a more enlightened society built on the principles of sustainability, peace, health, and dynamic action.

Website: **http://theshiftnetwork.com**

Michael Barrette	Ben Hart	Craig Kugel
Stephen Dinan	Emily Hine	Rebecca Bell Massoud
Michael DuBois	Jeffrey Kihn	Rev. Devaa Haley Mitchell
Deborah Dove Eudene		Alison Weeks

The Club of Budapest

The Club of Budapest is a global organization that was founded in 1993 by systems theorist and philosopher Dr. Ervin Laszlo. The mission for the Club of Budapest is to serve as a catalyst for the transformation to a sustainable world through the promotion of the emergence of a planetary consciousness. The club has a unique focus on integrating spirituality, science, and the arts; and interconnecting generations and cultures.

The Club of Budapest is dedicated to fostering learning communities worldwide that enhance the rapid development of a global consciousness, without which the world is unlikely to survive present economic, political, and societal challenges.

Website: **www.clubofbudapest.org**

The Club of Budapest International Foundation
Budapest Klub Alapítvány
1014 Budapest
Szentháromság tér 6
Hungary

Founder	International Trustees
Dr. Ervin Laszlo*	William Gladstone
	Gayle Newhouse

Honorary Members				
H. E. Oscar Arias	Vigdis Finnboga-dottir	H. E. Vaclav Havel	H. R. H. Irene van Lippe-Biesterfeld	H. E. Karan Singh
H. E. A. T. Ariyaratne	Milos Forman	Hazel Henderson	Shu-Hsien Liu	Sir Sigmund Sternberg
Karlheinz Bohm	Peter Gabriel	Jean Houston	Eva Marton	H. E. Rita Sussmuth

Raffi Cavoukian	H. E. Hans-Dietrich Genscher	Bianca Jagger	Federico Mayor	H. E. Desmond Tutu
Paulo Coelho	Rivka Golani	Miklos Jancso	Zubin Mehta	Liv Ullman
Mihaly Csikszent-mihalyi	H. E. Arpad Goncz	Ken-Ichiro Kobayashi	Edgar Mitchell	H. E. Richard von Weizsacker
H. H. the XIVth Dalai Lama	Dr. Jane Goodall	Gidon Kremer	Edgar Morin	Elie Wiesel
Waris Dirie	Krishna Gopala	Swami Kriyananda	Peter Russell	Betty Williams
Riane Eisler	H. E. Mikhail Gorbachev	Hans Kwng	Masami Saionji	Muhammad Yunus

*Dr. Laszlo wrote the book *WorldShift 2012* in 2009, which has inspired the creation of numerous WorldShift initiatives that operate independently in association with the Club of Budapest International.

WorldShift Community: **http://ervinlaszlo.com/worldshiftcommunity**

WorldShift 2012 (social network and campaign): **http://worldshift2012.org**

WorldShift Movement (Shift One Thing campaign): **www.worldshiftmovement.org**

WorldShift Council, the WorldShift 20 (an independent council to complement the conclusions of the G-20): **http://worldshiftcouncil.org**

Worldshift Media (media projects): **www.world shiftmedia.org**

WorldShift Network: **www.worldshiftnetwork.org**

Bioneers

Founded in 1990, Bioneers brings together social and scientific innovators from all disciplines to study, discuss, and disseminate solutions to major environmental and social issues. In 2008 more than 12,000 people attended the Bioneers Conference, connecting through a network of networks, with hundreds of thousands of people dedicated to creating positive change for a sustainable world.

Website: **www.bioneers.org**

> Bioneers, aka Collective Heritage Institute
> 1607 Paseo De Peralta, #3
> Santa Fe, NM 87501

Kenny Ausubel	Dune Lankard	Nina Simons
Charlotte Brody	Elizabeth Kapu'uwailani Lindsey	Hugo Steensma
Gay Dillingham	Chief Oren Lyons	Lynne Twist
Polly Howells	Melissa K. Nelson	Greg Watson
	David Orr	

APPENDIX E

Additional Resources

Books and Programs Created by Jack Canfield

The *Chicken Soup for the Soul*® series contains more than 225 titles, 60 of which have appeared on the *New York Times* and other bestseller lists. The titles from that series most relevant to the theme of this book are:

Canfield, Jack, and Mark Victor Hansen. *Chicken Soup for the Soul: 101 Stories to Open the Heart and*

Rekindle the Spirit. Deerfield Beach, FL: Health Communications, Inc., 1993.

————. *Chicken Soup for the Teacher's Soul: Stories to Open the Hearts and Rekindle the Spirits of Educators*. Deerfield Beach, FL: Health Communications, Inc., 2002.

Canfield, Jack, Mark Victor Hansen, and Amy Newmark. *Chicken Soup for the Soul: Think Positive: 101 Inspirational Stories about Counting Your Blessings and Having a Positive Attitude*. Cos Cob, CT: Chicken Soup for the Soul Publishing, LLC, 2010.

Canfield, Jack, Mark Victor Hansen, and LeAnn Thieman. *Chicken Soup for the Soul: A Book of Miracles: 101 True Stories of Healing, Faith, Divine Intervention, and Answered Prayers*. Cos Cob, CT: Chicken Soup for the Soul Publishing, LLC, 2010.

Canfield, Jack, Mark Victor Hansen, Candice C. Carter, Susanna Palomares, Linda K. Williams, and Bradley L. Winch. *Chicken Soup for the Soul: Stories for a Better World*. Deerfield Beach, FL: Health Communications, Inc., 2005.

Canfield, Jack, Mark Victor Hansen, Arline McGraw Oberst, John T. Boal, Tom Lagana, and Laura Lagana. *Chicken Soup for the Volunteer's Soul: Stories to Celebrate the Spirit of Courage, Caring and Community.* Deerfield Beach, FL: Health Communications, Inc., 2002.

Jack's other books include:

Canfield, Jack. *How to Get from Where You Are to Where You Want to Be: The 25 Principles of Success.* London: HarperElement, 2007.

Canfield, Jack, and Mark Victor Hansen, *Dare to Win.* New York: Berkley Books, 1994.

———. *The Aladdin Factor: How to Ask for and Get Everything You Want in Life.* New York: Berkley, 1995.

Canfield, Jack, Mark Victor Hansen, and Les Hewitt. *The Power of Focus: How to Hit Your Business, Personal and Financial Targets with Absolute Certainty.* Deerfield Beach, FL: Health Communications, Inc., 2000.

Canfield, Jack, Mark Victor Hansen, Jeanna Gabellini, and Eva Gregory. *Life Lessons for Mastering the Law of Attraction: 7 Essential Ingredients for Living a Prosperous Life.* Deerfield Beach, FL: Health Communications, Inc., 2008.

Canfield, Jack, and Kent Healy. *The Success Principles for Teens: How to Get from Where You Are to Where You Want to Be.* Deerfield Beach, FL: Health Communications, Inc., 2008.

Canfield, Jack, and Gay Hendricks. *You've GOT to Read This Book!: 55 People Tell the Story of the Book That Changed Their Life.* New York: William Morrow, 2006.

Canfield, Jack, and Janet Switzer. *The Success Principles: How to Get from Where You Are to Where You Want to Be.* New York: HarperCollins, 2005. Trade paperback edition, Collins, 2006.

Canfield, Jack, and D.D. Watkins. *Jack Canfield's Key to Living the Law of Attraction: A Simple Guide to Creating the Life of Your Dreams.* Deerfield Beach, FL: Health Communications, Inc., 2007.

———. *Gratitude: A Daily Journal.* Deerfield Beach, FL: Health Communications, Inc., 2007.

Other programs include:

The Success Principles: Your 30-Day Journey from Where You Are to Where You Want to Be. This is a 30-day audio course on 6 CDs, with a 98-page workbook. Santa Barbara, CA: The Canfield Training Institute, 2003. **www.jackcanfield.com**

The Success Principles (DVD). Produced by Better Life Media, 2006. **www.jackcanfield.com**

Effortless Success: Living the Law of Attraction. An 8-CD and workbook home study course on living the Law of Attraction. Minnetonka, MN: Learning Strategies Corporation, 2008. **www.jackcanfield.com**

Gaiam Portraits: Jack Canfield—Discover Your "Soul" Purpose (DVD). Produced by Gaiam, 2011. **www .jackcanfield.com**

Books and Programs Created by William Gladstone

Gladstone, William. *The Twelve.* New York, NY: Vanguard, 2009.

Gladstone, William, Richard Greninger, and John Selby. *Tapping the Source*. New York, NY: Sterling Publishing, 2010.

Gladstone, William, Richard Greninger, and Gayle Newhouse. *Tapping the Source* (DVD). Produced by Waterside Productions. 2010. **www.tappingthesource movie.com**

————. *Voices and Faces from the Source* DVD series **www.tappingthesourcemovie.com**

Gladstone, William, Gayle Newhouse, and John Woods. *Tapping the Source: The Original Course.* **www .tappingthesourcemovie.com**

Gladstone, William, Gayle Newhouse, and Clay Stevens. *Tapping the Source* The Game **www.tappingthe sourcemovie.com**

APPENDIX F

Books about the Phenomenon of 2012

These are just a few of the hundreds of books about 2012:

Argüelles, José. *The Mayan Factor: Path Beyond Technology.* Rochester, VT: Bear & Company, 1987.

————. *Manifesto for the Noosphere: The Next Stage in the Evolution of Human Consciousness.* Berkeley, CA: Evolver Editions, 2011.

Braden, Gregg, Peter Russell, Daneil Pinchbeck, et al. *The Mystery of 2012: Predictions, Prophecies, and Possibilities*. Louisville, CO: Sounds True Publishing, 2007. (Audio is also available.)

Christi, Nicolya. *2012: A Clarion Call: Your Soul's Purpose in Conscious Evolution*. Rochester, VT: Bear & Company, 2011.

Clow, Barbara Hand. *The Mayan Code: Time Acceleration and Awakening the World Mind*. Rochester, VT: Bear & Company, 2007.

Gladstone, William. *The Twelve*. New York, NY: Vanguard Press, 2009.

Jenkins, John Major, and Terence McKenna. *Maya Cosmogenisis 2010: The True Meaning of the Maya Calendar End-Date*. Rochester, VT: Bear & Company, 1998.

Melchizedek, Drunvalo. *Serpent of Light: Beyond 2012—the Movement of the Earth's Kundalini and the Rise of the Female Light, 1949 to 2013*. Newburyport, MA: Weiser Books, 2008.

Michell, John, and Christine Rhone. *Twelve-Tribe Nations: Sacred Number and the Golden Age*. Rochester, VT: Inner Traditions, 2008.

•

Page, Christine R. *2012 and the Galactic Center: The Return of the Great Mother.* Rochester, VT: Bear & Company, 2008.

South, Stephanie. *2012: Biography of a Time Traveler: The Journey of José Argüelles.* Franklin Lakes, NJ: Career Press, 2009.

Walsch, Neale Donald. *The Mother of Invention: The Legacy of Barbara Marx Hubbard and the Future of YOU!* Carlsbad, CA: Hay House, 2011.

APPENDIX G

Thomas Willhite's Motorcycle Training Course

Mr. Thomas D. Willhite co-founded PSI World Seminars in 1973, and developed a series of educational programs that enable PSI students to tap their full potential.

PSI teachings channel one's energies to be productive, to attain a life's ambition, to have better relationships, to live life to its fullest, and to create extraordinary achievements. With thousands of graduates all over the world, PSI World Seminars continues to change lives with this philosophy.

What follows are the first 13 points of Thomas's 107-point course on Motorcycle Maintenance and Riding skills. The full course is available as an e-book from **www.goldenmotorcyclegang.com** or **www .psiworldseminars.com**. There is much you can learn from this timeless advice, and it is just as valuable whether you ever intend to ride a motorcycle or not.

1. You are responsible for where you ride, how you ride, and where you finish.

2. You've got to set your position on the bike (your attitude) based on where you're at and where you want to go.

3. You've got to take care of your equipment.

4. Don't let your ego take you into an "event" you're not prepared for.

5. Anybody can ride in a straight line; it takes a lot more work to navigate through twists and turns and up and down hills and obstacles—the motorcycle is a metaphor for life.

6. You choose the fuel for your bike . . . good fuel makes it easier to drive.

7. The transmission is for "shifting" as required as you encounter different requirements for traveling.

8. You have to be aware of what you are keeping your eye on—the road ahead—because you will go where you set your sights.

9. If you practice more on your riding, you will ride better.

10. You are the only one who can ride your bike your way.

11. You've got to be prepared mentally and physically to ride the bike; any complacency or casualness will result in an accident—which is not what you want.

12. You want your bike to be impeccable—it was designed to do what you want . . . don't "put up" with the bike not being the way you want it.

13. Go over in your mind where you are going and how you are going to use the bike to get there.

ACKNOWLEDGMENTS

From Bill:

First and foremost, I want to thank my co-author, Jack Canfield. Jack not only told me the original Golden Motorcycle story more than a decade ago, but has been a wonderful writing partner. I have learned a great deal about the craft of storytelling from collaborating with Jack.

I also want to thank Gayle Newhouse, who has been my source of joy and inspiration for the last seven years. Living with Gayle is a constant delight, and her support has enabled me to focus on writing this book with clarity and calmness. Gayle also assisted in reading early drafts of the manuscript and providing her never-failing feminine instinct on presenting a balanced story and characters.

Others who shared their time and energy reviewing the manuscript included Stewart Emery, Jane Willhite, Andrew Cohen, Daniel Pinchbeck, Barnet Bain, and Barbara Marx Hubbard. Barbara is the co-star of our adventure, and she read the manuscript throughout its development, always offering specific suggestions that greatly improved the flow of the book's message about Conscious Evolution.

I also want to acknowledge our publisher, Reid Tracy of Hay House, and his excellent staff, including Jill Kramer, Shannon Littrell, Gail Gonzales, and Stacey Smith. Representing Waterside Productions, I would like to acknowledge Neil Gudovitz for his editorial contribution, and Kathleen Rushall and Taryn McCallan for their tireless keyboarding of the many drafts of the manuscript.

Writing a book and having it published in the best possible way is a journey that requires the efforts of many more people than I can name in these acknowledgments. To all of you, my thanks and appreciation for your ongoing efforts. And, of course, my appreciation for all of you who in your own way are members of the Golden Motorcycle Gang.

From Jack:

I first wish to acknowledge Bill Gladstone, who came up with the idea for sharing my Golden Motorcycle Gang experience. It never would have occurred to me without his encouragement. Bill also did a lot of the heavy lifting, turning our series of hour-long conversations and interviews into readable chapters and a coherent narrative.

Second, I wish to thank Barbara Marx Hubbard for her countless years of inspiration in my own life. I still remember sitting in an office in Santa Monica, California, in 1983 where she explained to all of the head trainers at Insight Training Seminars why we should support her candidacy for the vice-presidential nomination for the Democratic Party. That was 28 years ago!

Third, I wish to thank all of the people who worked hard in the beginning to co-create the Transformational Leadership Council, especially Marcia Martin, its first Executive Director; Pete Bissonnette, Hale Dwoskin, Marci Shimoff, Raymond Aaron, Donna Steinhorn, Stewart Emery, and Ivan Misner —all of whom have served on its Board of Directors; Robert MacPhee, its second Executive Director; and Guy Stickney, Tyson Young, Sidney Cresci, James Redmond, Mike Foster, and Shannon Mell, who have handled most of the logistical work in creating our amazing semiannual meetings over the years. I also want to thank fellow TLC'er and Co-founder of the Pachamama Alliance, Lynne Twist, for opening my eyes to think more ecologically and more globally.

Fourth, I would like to thank Patty Aubery, the president of the Canfield Training Group, for always having my back and overseeing the day-to-day operations of my company. She keeps me grounded in reality so that I always have a stable platform to pursue my visions and projects. And I could not do any of it without my amazing staff: Veronica Romero, Jesse Ianniello, Lisa Williams, Andrea Haefele, Sam Chillingworth, Teresa Collett, Alice Doughty, Heather Giddings, Katie Roth, and our timeless brilliant and always centered COO—Russ Kamalski.

Fifth, I want to thank my wife, Inga, who is my inspiration, my muse, and my mentor on what it means to be an authentically real and spontaneous human being while I strive to fulfill my higher sense of purpose. And thanks to my children—Oran, Kyle, and Christopher—for always modeling what following your own inner guidance and doing it your own way is all about . . . and to my stepchildren—Travis and Riley—for teaching me to appreciate diversity in all its forms.

And last, to all the people at Hay House who have championed and supported the project—from Reid Tracy to Jill Kramer and Shannon Littrell and Stacey Smith—thank you.

ABOUT THE AUTHORS

Jack Canfield is the co-author of the #1 *New York Times* best-selling *Chicken Soup for the Soul* series, which has sold more than 500 million copies in 47 languages. Known as America's #1 Success Coach, he is also the author of *The Success Principles, The Aladdin Factor, Dare to Win, The Key to Living the Law of Attraction,* and *The Power of Focus.* Jack is a featured teacher in the movies *The Secret* and *Tapping the Source;* and has appeared on more than 1,000 radio and television programs, including *The Oprah Winfrey Show, Montel, Larry King Live,* and the *Today* show.

Jack is the CEO of the Canfield Training Group and the founder of the Transformational Leadership Council. He is a graduate of Harvard University and the University of Massachusetts; and lives with his wife, Inga, in Santa Barbara, California.

Website: **www.JackCanfield.com**

As an author, **William Gladstone** is best known for his international bestseller *The Twelve*. He is also the co-author of *Tapping the Source* and co-producer of the film of the same name. William has an undergraduate degree from Yale University and a graduate degree in cultural anthropology from Harvard University.

As a literary agent and the founder of Waterside Productions, William represents luminaries such as Eckhart Tolle, Thom Hartmann, and Neale Donald Walsch. He is a trustee of the International Club of Budapest and has served as the founding alumni president for Schoolyear Abroad. William resides in Cardiff-by-the-Sea, California.

Website: **www.waterside.com**

We hope you enjoyed this Hay House book. If you'd like
to receive our online catalog featuring additional information
on Hay House books and products, or if you'd like to find
out more about the Hay Foundation, please contact:

Hay House, Inc., P.O. Box 5100, Carlsbad, CA 92018-5100
(760) 431-7695 or (800) 654-5126
(760) 431-6948 (fax) or (800) 650-5115 (fax)
www.hayhouse.com® • **www.hayfoundation.org**

Published and distributed in Australia by: Hay House Australia
Pty. Ltd., 18/36 Ralph St., Alexandria NSW 2015 • *Phone:*
612-9669-4299 • *Fax:* 612-9669-4144 • www.hayhouse.com.au

Published and distributed in the United Kingdom by:
Hay House UK, Ltd., 292B Kensal Rd., London W10 5BE • *Phone:*
44-20-8962-1230 • *Fax:* 44-20-8962-1239 • www.hayhouse.co.uk

Published and distributed in the Republic of South Africa by:
Hay House SA (Pty), Ltd., P.O. Box 990, Witkoppen 2068
Phone/Fax: 27-11-467-8904 • www.hayhouse.co.za

Published in India by: Hay House Publishers India, Muskaan
Complex, Plot No. 3, B-2, Vasant Kunj, New Delhi 110 070 • *Phone:*
91-11-4176-1620 • *Fax:* 91-11-4176-1630 • www.hayhouse.co.in

Distributed in Canada by: Raincoast, 9050 Shaughnessy St.,
Vancouver, B.C. V6P 6E5 • *Phone:* (604) 323-7100
Fax: (604) 323-2600 • www.raincoast.com

Take Your Soul on a Vacation

Visit **www.HealYourLife.com®** to regroup,
recharge, and reconnect with your own magnificence.
Featuring blogs, mind-body-spirit news, and life-
changing wisdom from Louise Hay and friends.

Visit **www.HealYourLife.com** today!